THE MAKING OF A
TRAILBLAZER

OVERCOME YOUR PAIN * IGNITE YOUR PATH
EMBRACE YOUR PURPOSE

RICHARD HORNE JR
FOREWORD BY GOD

DEDICATION

This book is dedicated to my Lord and Savior Jesus Christ. I love and appreciate you for using my setbacks as a launching pad to catapult me toward the purpose and plan you ordained for my life. I simply cannot thank you enough for all you have done, are doing, and will do in and through my life to be a blessing to my wife, children, family and countless others. To You Lord I give all glory, honor and praise. You are faithful and truly amazing!

ACKNOWLEDGEMENTS

I want to first give thanks to God for sending His only begotten Son into this world to save us from sin and death. I am honored He has chosen me to be the gleaner of 'blessed' seeds that I continuously reap from to this day.

To my beautiful wife Renda, you surely are the love of my life! You are a devoted wife, mother, grandmother, minister, author, nurse and my very best friend. I thank you for always honoring the covenant we made together before God, and continuing to love me through good times and bad. I appreciate the fact that no matter what happened during my development, you refused to give up on me. I can always count on you to remain steadfast in prayer with and for me. God used you to save my life, give me a family, encourage, support, and help me bring forth this book. The word of God says in Proverbs 18:22, *"The man who finds a wife finds a treasure, and he receives favor from the Lord"* (NLT). It is my pleasure to share my life's journey with you – my treasure. I love you Baby!

To my children Brandon, Rockell, Blake, Kiya, Kristen, Renda, Rachel, Ri'Char, and my grandchildren – I love you all very much. You probably do not realize how instrumental you all were in saving my life. It was my love for you and my appreciation to God for allowing me to look at your faces every day, which helped to keep me moving in the right direction. Thanks for believing in me and always pushing me to do better. You all are such a blessing and great source of inspiration for me. I release God's blessings over your lives.

I want to give thanks to my father Richard A. Horne Sr. and my mother Sharon A. Horne (deceased), I love you both very much. Despite some "rough patches" in the past, I am grateful for your love and I honor you as my parents. It was during those tough times that I found my Lord and Savior Jesus Christ. Dad, I am so grateful to God for the bond and close relationship we share. You have been and always will be an inspiration to me. Mom, I am so grateful to God for restoring our relationship prior to your passing. If I could have kept you here with me another thirty years, that would not have been long enough. There is not a day that goes by that I do not miss you.

To my Mother-in-law Pastor Teola Funches, your energy and strength amazes me. If it were not for you, I would not have my wife Renda. The contribution of strength, love, and faith you instilled in her is a continuous blessing. I love, appreciate, and thank you.

To my siblings Norman, Tracey, and Stacey, thanks for your love, encouragement and support. Despite our ups and downs throughout the years, our love for one another has never wavered. Our close relationships with one another is a testament to our strength and unconditional love. You guys are priceless to me and I love you. I would also like to extend my thanks and appreciation to my siblings-in-law.

I would like to thank Apostle Jose De La Rosa and Pastor Keila De La Rosa of World Christian Center International in Buford, GA. My family and I love and appreciate you. In addition, I would like to thank Apostle Lennell D. Caldwell and his beautiful wife Dr. Carol Caldwell of First Baptist World Changers International Ministries in Detroit, MI. You both have been very instrumental in my spiritual development and maturity in the Word of God. Thank you for teaching on holiness, being true examples, and preparing me and my family to "blaze the trails" God prepared for us to become World Changers.

Mrs. Kurland-Simpson and Mrs. A. Simpson, you two played a vital role in my being alive today. God used you two beautiful angels to save my life on numerous occasions! You were there for me when I had no one to turn to, and did for me when no one else would. Because of you, I am able to write my book now, instead of others having to write my obituary back then. THANK YOU, I LOVE YOU and GOD BLESS YOU BOTH TREMENDOUSLY ON THIS SIDE OF HEAVEN AND BEYOND.

I would like to personally thank my friends Ray and Charisse Mills. Thank you, Juan and LaTrese Forest and Mr. John Reed for your encouragement and support. Aaron Funches, you are not just my brother-in-law, but my friend as well. Thanks for your support, encouragement, and simply being there whenever I need you. Thanks you Dr. Arthur I. Bouchier, for being an inspiration, teacher, supporter, and friend. Your humility and strength is a testament to your anointed ministry.

TABLE OF CONTENTS

FOREWORD BY GOD

For I know the plans I have for you, says the Lord. They are plans for good and not for disaster, to give you a future and a hope. My child, listen to me and do as I say, and you will have a long, good life. I will teach you wisdom's ways and lead you in straight paths. When you walk, you won't be held back; when you run, you won't stumble. Take hold of my instructions; don't let them go. Guard them, for they are the key to life. Guard your heart above all else, for it determines the course of your life. Look straight ahead, and fix your eyes on what lies before you. Mark out a straight path for your feet; stay on the safe path. Don't get sidetracked; keep your feet from following evil. Let your light so shine before men, that they may see your good works, and glorify your Father which is in heaven (Jeremiah 29:11 NLT, Proverbs 4:10-13, 23, 25-27 NLT, Matthew 5:16 KJV).

God
Creator of the universe
(Trailblazer Originator)

THE MAKING OF A TRAILBLAZER

CHAPTER 1

FOUNDATION, FEATURES, FACTS,

AND FALSEHOODS

FOUNDATION

Throughout the years there have been several songs that refer to man being "only human." There is one song in particular titled *I'm Only Human*, sang by the group *Human League* that says, "*I'm only human, of flesh and blood, a man. Human, born to make mistakes.*" However, nothing could be further from the truth! The bible clearly gives our foundational origin and purpose in the following scripture in Genesis, 1:26-28, *Then God said, "Let us make human beings in our image, to be like us. They will reign over the fish in the sea, the birds in the sky, the livestock, all the wild animals on the earth, and the small animals that scurry along the ground. (27) So God created human beings in his own image. In the image of God he created them; male and female he created them. (28) Then God blessed them and said, "Be fruitful and multiply. Fill the earth and govern it. Reign over the fish in the sea, the birds in the sky, and all the animals that scurry along the ground."*

We know that God is a Spirit (John 4:24). And so, man was brought into existence to be a tangible, visual representation of God's spiritual form in the earth. We, both male and female were produced as the physical portrait of God and given power to exercise complete control over the earth and everything in it. In addition, God empowered man to prosper and instructed them to reproduce and fill the earth with the image He and man shared.

The human part or "outer shell" of man was formed from the dust of the ground, but man did not receive "life" until the spirit part of man was breathed into him by God. This is demonstrated in the following scripture, *"then the Lord God formed the man from the dust of the ground. He breathed the breath of life into the man's nostrils, and the man became a living person"* (Genesis 1:7 NLT). So technically, it is when man is without his spirit that he is really "only human." However, we will dig deeper into this in an upcoming chapter.

A "**Trailblazer**" *is one who ignites a path through terrain (a field of knowledge or interest) in order to fulfill his or her purpose, and make a clear path for others to follow.* The very first trailblazer was God Himself, and He planned for man to shadow His path of success. Take note that man was the only creation by God that He created in His own image, breathed life into, and gave authority to rule over everything on the earth. He instructed man to *"prosper, reproduce, fill earth, and take charge,"* (Genesis 1:28 MSG). This is because man was created in the earth in God's image to "mirror" what God is and does in Heaven.

God created the world by using his powerful words to produce it. He then led Adam to reproduce that same power in the earth by naming all of the animals (Genesis 1:19). It still blows my mind to think of how God created all the animals, yet waited until He created Adam and gave him authority to name them. In a sense, this was the beginning of Adam transitioning into his role as a transformer, world changer, life transition specialist, and ultimately a trailblazer.

There are many notable trailblazers throughout history who have contributed to transforming the world in some form or another. Most of which we continue to benefit from to this day. If I had to list them all, as you probably know, it would go on and on and will continue so throughout our lifetime. This is because we humans were designed and instructed to do so from the very beginning of our existence.

When I speak of man being designed and instructed to transform the world from the beginning of our existence, I am not referring to the day we were birthed from our mother's womb, but the day we were conceived in the mind of God. The bible states in Jeremiah 1:5, how God explained to Jeremiah that He designed him and *knew what he was purposed to do in the earth **before** He created Jeremiah in his mother's womb. God continues telling Jeremiah that **before** he was born, God set him apart and appointed him as His prophet to the nations* (NLT, emphasis added). All human beings, both male and female, are to fulfill God's **overall** plan to impact the world with and for the glory of God. In addition, God has also designed an individual purpose and plan for each of us to fulfill by way of reproducing His image, authority and power in the earth, as it is in Heaven.

Our individual purpose is like a single puzzle piece. Although its shape may look similar to another piece, it is an original. It has its own unique design and independent roll it will play. Its frame cannot be altered in any way. To attempt to do so would not only distort its identity, but also affect the other pieces and alter the outcome of the overall picture. The streaks of color and odd designs that cover the single piece is only a fragment of what it entails. Alone, it may appear weak, minor or insignificant, but nothing could be further from the truth. It encompasses an unparalleled strength to influence as an extension of its creator.

For a time, the single piece may move around and attempt to settle in spaces that are too large or too small for it to fit into. The uncomfortable experiences of rejection and alienation may provoke the single piece to question if there really is a place for it at all in the enormous puzzle. But despite setbacks, the single piece continues on. Once the piece discovers and settles into its appointed position and joins with another piece, and yet another, and continues on until there are no empty spaces; it is then and only then, that it fulfills its purpose to complete a much bigger picture and impact change. In other words, God created every man as an individual vehicle for His purpose in the earth. We are to be an extension of Himself reflected in the earth.

FEATURES

The following are features (an interesting or important part, quality, ability, etc.) of a trailblazer:

> - Original (a person who is different from other people in an appealing or interesting way.)
> - Innovative (using new ideas or introducing new methods about how something can be done.)
> - Focused (on the plan of God for his or her life)
> - Fearless (not afraid, very brave)
> - Relentless (promising no abatement of severity, intensity, strength, or pace.)
> - Faithful (having or showing true and constant support or loyalty)

A Trailblazer is not an attention seeker! In fact, he or she does not have to do one thing to get attention. Trailblazers possess their own unique characteristics and features that individualizes and puts them in a class all by themselves. They recognize their features, understand their ability, and know their value. Furthermore, they are fearless and learn to master their God-given anointing to attract and influence the biggest, scariest sceptics on the face of the earth! Where others tend to give up or faint, is where they seem to pick up speed. They tend to go where others will not. They forgive the unforgiveable, and love the unlovable because they understand that love and forgiveness are the two greatest weapons of their artillery.

When it comes to trailblazers; losing is not never an option. They are victorious and will not give attention to anything contrary. Because trailblazers are purpose-driven and faith focused, their enemy's arrogant attitude and evil actions have a tendency to be ineffective in discouraging them. Proverbs 18:21 says, *Death and life are in the power of the tongue* (KJV), therefore, Trailblazers establish and follow a habit of trusting God's word no matter what! They *"walk by faith and not by sight"* as it states in 2nd Corinthians 5:7. This is because no matter how things look, what they hear, what others think, or what sceptics say; trailblazer's faith in God's word always has, and always will supersede all other's words.

FACTS

Jesus stated that man shall not (will not be able) to live by bread (physical, tangible food) alone, but by EVERY word (spiritual food) that is spoken by God Himself (Matthew 4:4). Being the trailblazer that He is, and living as a human being on the earth Jesus did just that. His success in doing so made it possible for all human beings to live victorious over his or her flesh and sin nature. Furthermore, Jesus was always focused, disciplined, obedient, and consistent when it came to walking out His purpose to redeem man from sin, death and hell, and stand as man's model of a "true" Trailblazer. Here are some facts to validate his "trailblazer" characteristics that are irrefutable:

- ➤ Jesus ALWAYS embraced His individuality, yet remained a team player (Matt 17:24-27, John 15:1-5).
- ➤ Jesus ALWAYS walked in faith and confidence, yet remained humble (Matthew 8:5-9, 13, John 14:10)
- ➤ Jesus ALWAYS respected and followed the will of God the Father, and not His own agenda (Matt 26:39).

- Jesus ALWAYS walked in love, compassion and gratitude (Luke 15:1-7, 10, Matthew 14:14-21, Matthew 15:32-38).
- Jesus was ALWAYS a respecter of the will of God the Father, and not a respecter of any particular group, clique, family member or person (Luke 8:19-21, Matthew 15-12-14).
- Jesus ALWAYS boldly spoke the truth in wisdom despite the danger He faced (Matthew 15:10-14, Luke 20:20-47).

The previous facts validate Jesus as the foundation in which every trailblazer should build there foundation upon. Believing in God is important, but it is only the beginning. Think about it. satan, demons, and fallen angels believe in God too. Therefore we know that only "believing" is not enough. We must move much further beyond belief only, and also trust Him as our Father, Savior, Teacher, Author of our purpose, and GPS to our destiny.

In conclusion, these facts have been validated repeatedly in the scriptures, as well as in the lives of believers to this day. I myself, as well as my family have experienced it for ourselves and can attest to it. In order to make progress in the direction in which God is leading, you are to mature and grow your faith by reading and listening to God's word (Romans 10:17). You must then activate His principles and use them as tools for daily living, as you blaze the path God predestined for you. To do so will provide continuous strength to sustain you along the journey, and lead you to a rewarding finish.

FALSEHOODS

Now that I have given you the foundation, features, and facts, I must also expose and dispel the falsehoods. Unfortunately, many tend to unintentionally get facts and falsehoods mixed up because they often look similar such as the following:

➢ RELIGION VS RELATIONSHIP - *Religion* is often mistaken for relationship, but the two are very different. Religion is an organized system or beliefs, ceremonies, and rules used to worship. However, "true" worship, sincerity and accountability is not required. Religion often lacks genuine structure and substance, and only requires one participant lacking a connection or interaction between two or more participants. It often involves methodology among people without truly interacting with God (i.e. Pharisees and Sadducees). *Relationship* is the way in which two or more people or things are connected or interact. It is a quality or state of being kin or family, and requires two or more participants. It is the Greek word *"koinonia"* meaning *"a companion, a partner or a joint-owner"* (i.e. a personal relationship with Jesus Christ).

➢ *THRILL SEEKERS VS REAL SEEKERS* – **"Thrill" Seekers** are those who look to fulfill their own agenda for their life and not God's. They walk by feelings and omit faith. They are unstable. They tend to be easily offended, and are artificial and fraudulent drifters. They believe in God's existence, but not all of His word. They have a form of godliness, but deny God's power. When it comes to thrill seekers, it is all about presentation (i.e. Judas). **"Real" Seekers** are those who look for God's will for their lives and not their own. They walk by faith, and do not focus on feelings. They are strong and stable in the faith. They are authentic and purpose driven followers who genuinely love God for who He is, and wholeheartedly seek Him without ulterior motives (i.e. Apostle Paul).

➤ FLICKERS VS FLAMES – **Flickers** are those who burn or glow in an unsteady way, producing an unsteady light. Their appearance and exit is swift as a flash of light because they lack stability (i.e. Thomas). **Flames** shine brightly. They display brilliance. They exhibit zeal, passion and stability. The word of God says in Matthew 5:16, "*Let your light so shine before men, and glorify your Father which is in heaven.*" Take note it never once said "let your light flicker" (i.e. Joseph).

➤ CONCEIT VS CONFIDENCE – **Conceit** is an excessive appreciation of one's own worth or virtue (i.e. pride). **Confidence** - a feeling or belief that you can do something well or succeed at something. Hebrews 10:35, "*So do not throw away this confident trust in the Lord. Remember the great reward it brings you*" (i.e. Abraham).

There are some that may be reading this in the privacy of your own space and saying, *"That sounds like me!"* If this relates to you and you recognize the presence of the preceding falsehoods reigning in one or more areas in your life, do not panic, feel embarrassed, get offended, or choose to ignore it any longer. Right now is your time to repent, turn from it and ask the Holy Spirit (your helper) to strengthen you and help you grow.

NOTES

CHAPTER 2

"D" DAY

The day had finally come. This would be the last court hearing regarding my parents' divorce. Surprisingly, they had managed to remain together in the same house without killing one another before their final court appearance. My three siblings and I were told we had to go along with our parents to court. I, a twelve-year-old kid at the time, was okay with it. I thought it would end all the contention in our house.

We all walked into the courtroom. I did not know what to expect. Imagine my surprise when the judge asked each of us point blank, *"Who would you like to live with?"* I did not hesitate or stutter as I said, *"I want to live with my Daddy."* Although I did not expect to be asked that question openly in front of everyone in the courtroom, it was not a difficult decision for me to make. In fact, I had already made my decision long before I entered that courtroom. It was the relationship, or lack of relationship that I had with each of my parents which progressed over the years, and played a part in guiding me with the decision I would make that day.

My parents were young when they had their first child prior to getting married. My mother would end up pregnant five times (miscarrying one of those children) in six years. For years, she worked two or three jobs simultaneously to help support her family. I hardly ever saw her because she seemed to always be at work. And when she was home, she complained a lot and often seemed upset. For her, the marriage had happened too quickly, the children had come too fast and frequent, and it all was simply too much for her to balance. Although she had been a generous person who had made it a priority to take care of her family and look out for others, it came a time when she decided she was going to look out for herself first. She felt as though there were things she was missing out on because of all the responsibility she had taken on. Therefore, the divorce was a way of freeing herself to enjoy her life while she was still young. She appeared to be a young, unhappy, overwhelmed, struggling wife and mother of four, in search of her youthful years she had surrendered way to soon.

My father was a hard worker who rarely missed work, but had challenges with his finances. To my knowledge, neither of my parents had a personal relationship with Jesus Christ during that time. Nor do I remember either of them consistently attending church. As a child, the relationship I had with each of my parents was like night and day. My relationship with my mother was strained. She worked a lot, so she did not spend much time with me. It probably would have been easier for me to count the days I saw her rather than the days I didn't. When we were together, it was uncomfortable talking to her. She was often verbally abusive and would belittle me. She would tell me things like, *"You act just like your daddy! I can't stand him, and I can't stand you! You're going to be no good just like him!"* Just hearing my father's name seemed to make her angry, which is why I never did understand why she named me after him. It would not surprise me if being Richard Jr may have contributed to what appeared to be her strong dislike for me as a child. For that reason, I never felt nurtured and loved by my mother during that time; only tolerated.

On the other hand, my father and I were close. He was sure to spend time with me, often listening to me express how I was feeling. Even though he did not provide many solutions to my concerns, he encouraged me and made sure I knew he loved and cared about me enough to listen. Although my family environment was somewhat dysfunctional, my father seemed to make me a priority at least some of the time. That is the reason I chose to live with him. Both my parents seemed stubborn and unapologetic in my opinion. Although some people may view divorce as a logical decision, as for me, divorce turned out to be a devastating blow that caused my world to fall apart.

In hind sight, my devastation did not appear to stem from divorce as much as it did from the aftermath. It would bring unimaginable hurt, pain, poverty, rejection, abuse, loss, separation, and abandonment to envelope my life and derail my future. As odd as it may sound, I believe my parents thought their divorce would bring closure and peace not only to them, but to my siblings and me as well. But nothing could be further from the truth. My parents really were clueless as to how that decision would turn my world upside down. But God had a plan for my life that would ultimately prevail. Just as fast as the court hearing began; it was over. My mother stated that she would leave the house to my father and move out.

THE AFTERMATH

My brother and one of my sisters went to live with my mother. My other sister and I stayed with my father. I did not know it then, but that would be the last time I would live with my mother. Eventually, my maternal grandparents took in one of my sisters to live with them. An aunt and uncle took in my other sister to live with them. My brother remained with my mother. I, on the other hand, did not go to live with any family or relatives and stayed with my father. Apparently, our family and relatives felt that I would be too much trouble and made it clear that they would not take me in. At that time, my siblings and I had issues we were dealing with. For me, it was bad decision making; which was due to a lack of positive guidance. I emulated the actions (mostly negative) of the older kids in my neighborhood. With my father mostly gone, I rarely received any discipline.

I developed the "thick skin" I felt I needed for survival, and pretty much did what I wanted to do. But on the flip side of that, I longed for a positive mentor to hold me accountable, and help steer me in the right direction. I wanted someone to step up and offer to help me. I wanted to hear words of encouragement, but instead I heard things like, *"Boy, you are bad, and you will always be bad! You will never change!"* I wanted to be accepted and given a chance just like my siblings. But no one volunteered to take me in. In fact, their blatant and swift rejection prompted me to ask myself, *"What is so wrong with me that no one wants me?"* As a kid, it hurt.

Ultimately, we ended up homeless. We pretty much slept wherever we could to avoid sleeping in the streets – literally. At that time, things were pretty tough! When I was about thirteen, my dad and I went our separate ways. Not only was I homeless, but alone as well.

There I was a homeless kid with no parents, no siblings, and no family to turn to. During that time, I didn't have many friends. Those few I considered friends managed to sneak me into their homes or garages after their parents were asleep, so that I could have a warm place to sleep. They were not allowed to play with me, because their parents felt I was a bad influence and would not amount to anything.

I slept in abandoned buildings, garages, vacant homes, and even on top of buildings when the weather permitted. There were countless days and nights that I spent all alone, but ironically, I wasn't very fearful. Despite that I was only a "tween," it was obvious no one else was going to take care of me. So, I made up in my mind that I would do what I felt I had to do to survive. At least that is what I thought. But it was more than that.

At age twelve, I started stealing food from local stores just to eat. I did not have any money, and food was scarce. For me to eat once a day was challenging. Therefore, eating three times a day was a miracle. Those were truly desperate times for me, and it was at those times that I turned to what I saw as desperate measures. I would make sandwiches, drink juice, and eat snacks out of the grocery cart I piled food into as I rolled it up and down each isle in the grocery store. Once I finished, I would then leave the cart with its partially eaten contents in the store. That was the beginning of a very slippery slope!

Food, among other necessities; was scarce. I had virtually no clothes, and maybe one pair of shoes. To make matters worse, I had no coat during the fall and winter months; not even a jacket. There were days and nights when I literally thought I was going to freeze! I remember my friend and me walking the streets one cold day, when I noticed this kid coming out of my old middle school. He immediately got my attention because he didn't just have on any coat, but a Max Julian! I pulled out a Beebe gun I carried around with me, and pointed it at him. I then demanded his coat, in which he quickly gave up without a fight. I immediately put it on as my friend and I ran our separate ways. It was only a few hours later when the police caught up with me while I was still wearing the coat. My plan involved getting me a coat; period! I never considered getting caught, or what that could possible entail. Although I hadn't mapped out my life for the following year, or even the following week in advance; this was not at all what I had anticipated. The plan sounded pretty simple, yet turned out to be anything but!

In the bible, Job 5: 12 states, *"He frustrates the plans of schemers so the work of their hands will not succeed"* (NLT). That was most certainly my current situation at that time. It did not matter that I was only fourteen years old, and the weapon was a Beebe gun. I committed my first armed robbery that day, which landed me in juvenile.

Dealing with a Double-Edged Sword

Before going to juvenile, I had been without any guidance and taking care of myself for quite a while. I was able to come and go as I pleased. Therefore, the last thing I wanted was to go from being free to roam the streets to being locked up, confined, and alienated to a cell. Then again, when I was on the streets I was often frustrated because I didn't have anywhere to go. So, believe it or not, going to Juvenile actually brought me some relief. At least there I had someone looking after me. I didn't have to worry about where I would sleep, or where my next meal would come from. I didn't have to be concerned with how hot or cold the weather would be, because I didn't have to live on the streets anymore – at least for a while. What I considered my biggest concern while living on the streets was now my biggest relief. I would definitely have something to eat at least three times a day for the next two months without having to steal it. As a fourteen-year-old kid, I would also get the accountability I secretly longed for yet lacked.

During those two months in juvenile, I didn't receive any letters, not one visitor, or any communication from anyone; including my parents and family. Although I was disappointed, I was not angry, bitter, or resentful. That was because I understood that it was my own bad decisions that landed me there. Also, I never really was a grudge-holding type of person either. I looked forward to the day that I could get out of jail, and put everything behind.

The day in which I would be released from juvenile was fast approaching, and reality started to set in. Although I dreamed of a fresh start, I had four things that started to weigh heavily on me.

> ➢ I had not communicated with anyone.
> ➢ I only had a week or so left of my sentence.
> ➢ It was the middle of winter.
> ➢ I had nowhere to go.

Prior to my "going home," there was no meeting with a social worker or anyone else to make sure I would have a home to go to. There were no meeting-of-the-minds to gather resources for a fourteen-year-old kid whom had not received one letter, one visitor, or any communication during the entire two months he was in juvenile. Technically, there was pretty much nothing in place to prevent me from re-entering the very environment that attributed to me going to juvenile in the first place. I have to admit it was scary.

My "going home" day had arrived. I was given $15.00 and a brief "good luck" speech by the juvenile justice system, before being sent on my way. That was it; nothing more – nothing less. Although I had no idea where I was going, I had made up in mind I would somehow survive!

I will never forget how extremely cold that winter day was! As I made numerous calls from pay phones, my body shivered continuously from the frigid low temperature, wind, and blowing snow. Unable to reach my father and other family members by phone, I eventually got in touch with one of my sisters. She gave me the phone number for my mother. When I called my mother and told her I had been released from juvenile, she did not sound glad, enthused or even relieved. Her voice remained monotone. I proceeded to tell her that I was very cold, and had nowhere to go. She told me where she lived before the call ended, so I took the last of what remained of the $15.00 I was given, and rode a bus to where she lived at the time.

When I arrived at her house, I knocked on her door. She opened the door, but kept the screen door remained shut. I was so relieved to see her! I had hoped she would invite me in, hug me, let me know she was there for me, and that everything would be okay. But it was right at that moment I heard a deep male voice barrel out the words, *"Who the (bleep) is at my door!"* She then replied, *"It's my son."* The deep male voice then replied, *"I don't give a (bleep) who it is, close my door!"* I looked at my mother and said, *"I don't have anywhere to go, and its cold out here."* She told me to hold on a minute, before briefly shutting the door. She returned and gave me $5.00 and said, *"My boyfriend said you can't stay here."* She then shut the door completely. I was so hurt. I was so upset and cried as I walked away. There I was, fourteen years old, cold, and homeless. My sadness was not a result of her rejection, because I was used to it, and somewhat expected it. It was due to the immediate and painful reality that I would have to survive the brutally cold weather, without any shelter or money, and without knowing exactly how.

With no back-up plan and not knowing what I would do throughout that day, I took the $5.00 my mother had given me, and I got on the Grand River bus that evening, and rode it until the bus driver had come to the end of that route. He then told me it was the end of the route and it was time for me to get off. I decided to be open and honest with the bus driver. I proceeded to share with him that I was homeless, had nowhere to go and I was cold, and I asked if I could ride the bus throughout his shift that night. He had compassion for me and agreed. He also bought me something to eat during that night as well. The next morning at the end of his shift, he wished me well as I exited the bus.

Touched by my Angels

Even when I felt alone, I somehow knew I was not alone. I now know God was covering and protecting me. That following morning, having nowhere to turn, I called my probation officer. We will call her Angel. I told her my situation, and instead of turning me away as everyone else had; she helped me tremendously! God used Angel and her mother-in-law to save my life more times than I could count.

These two ladies looked beyond my horrible reputation and criminal record, and shared the love of God with me. Angel's mother-in-law treated me as her godson and began speaking the word of God over my life. Despite how many times I messed up, she was relentless in claiming me for the Kingdom of God. Frankly, these ladies did <u>exactly</u> as the bible states in Matthew 25:35-40, "*I was hungry, and you fed me. I was thirsty, and you gave me drink. I was a stranger, and you invited me into your home. I was naked, and you gave me clothing. I was sick, and you cared for me. I was in prison, and you visited me*" (NLT version, emphasis added). Without the clothes, food, shelter, visits, care, encouragement, prayers, and unconditional love they extended to me as an "at risk" teen, I do not believe I would have survived to see my twenties.

I was released from Juvenile at age seventeen. Within a couple of months, I landed myself in prison for armed robbery. That is when I also received the surprising news that a young lady I had been seeing was pregnant, and I would soon become a father. The news was both scary and confusing. On one hand, I pondered over how I would take care of a child. On the other hand, I thought of how I was abandoned and left to fin for myself as a young child and I did not want that for any child of mine.

Although I knew I had done wrong by committing crimes and would have to deal with the consequences of my actions; I was crushed! Not just for myself, but also for the child I would be inadvertently abandoning. I was subconsciously repeating a demonic cycle that seemed to have had a death grip on my family. I too had become accustomed to accepting temporary remedies for my chronic problem – pain!

I had been in so much mental, emotional and spiritual pain for so long; it became somewhat normal to me. I was in serious need of uprooting my pain and receiving complete healing. Technically, I only had two options. The first would be to humble myself, get help, and change my path. The second would be to prepare myself for life in prison or even worse – death!

NOTES

_____

_____

_____

_____

_____

_____

_____

_____

_____

_____

_____

_____

_____

_____

CHAPTER 3

OVERCOME YOUR PAIN

During the first six months of my prison sentence, my son Brandon was born. It was torture not being able to be there at his birth. There would be no holding or touching him. I could not even see him. I could only dream about the day I would be able to see, hold, and touch my son. Although I put up a good front for the inmates around me, I was heartbroken and my spirit was low. *"How could I have gotten myself in this position,"* I often thought. It was at this time that the haunting voices of those who claimed that I would never amount to anything constantly rang in my ears. But then the sound of my godmother's voice praying and confessing empowerment over my life would briefly comfort and encourage me.

Days turned into weeks, and weeks turned into months. No phone calls, no visits, and no letters from my family. Many of them felt I deserved to be incarcerated and forgotten. But not Mrs. Kurland-Simpson and her mother-in-law. Those two angels made themselves available and were always a blessing to me. Again, I must reiterate how they exemplified Matthew 25:35-40. I do not know if anyone would ever grasp how much their love and kindness meant to me. Every phone call, letter, and visit gave me hope and kept me going. At the time it truly was everything to me and really all I had left.

Receiving pictures of my newborn son also seemed to turn things around for me. Those pictures lifted my spirit and gave me hope at a time when anything positive looked impossible for me. However, the moments of elation were mostly temporal. Despite any attempts to remain hopeful, it seemed the pain of my past was always present. It was not that I could not put the past behind me, it was that I simply did not want to do so because it was all I knew. Not only was I a prisoner doing time, but I was also a prisoner in time!

From the time I was young up until my incarceration, I felt I had been given a raw deal, robbed, and cheated by my parents and forgotten about by my family, and the system. Physically I was in prison, yet mentally and spiritually I was in a lot of pain. As I sat in my cell, I remember often thinking to myself I will never mount up to much, because that is what everyone else said about me. I felt worthless and unloved. My pain was so intense at times it became the center of my existence. Sadly, I allowed the pain of my past to dominate my present, and smother the hope of my future. More and more I began looking back and meditating on where I had come from. This was because I did not think I had anything or anyone to look forward to.

Looking back now, I was so full of myself! For me, it was all about what had, or had not, been done for me, or to me. I knew I had done wrong and it was my bad choices and actions that landed me where I was, but I chose not to focus on that part of me. I only wanted to focus on the part of me that had been victimized – not me being the victimizer. I thought about all of the terrible things I had suffered from others, and not about all the terrible sufferings I caused others. I felt as though God had forgotten me and was not concerned with what happened to me or how badly my life was going. I believed I had been denied several opportunities at a better childhood and ultimately a better life. This fractured way of thinking lead me to become an opportunist – *someone who tries to get an advantage or something valuable from a situation without thinking*

about what is fair or right (Merrian-Webster Dictionary).
Simply put – I was selfish!

I also had major trust issues. I barely trusted Mrs.
Kurland-Simpson and Mrs. Simpson, but outside of them I
virtually trusted no one. It seemed as though anyone I put
my trust in always let me down. As a result, I did not
believe God. I do not want you to get this twisted, I
believed in God, but I did not believe God. There is a huge
difference between the two! To believe in God is to
believe that He exists, but does not mean one trusts His
word or ability. Although I had been introduced or
exposed to God in my youth, I had failed to get to know
him personally and establish a relationship with Him. I did
not attend church and hear the word or read the bible,
therefore I had no faith in God or what He was capable of
doing in and through my life. I only walked by sight, what I
could see; not by faith. I had things twisted in my head
and my heart and that is the way I lived as the following
scripture confirms, *"For as he thinketh in his heart, so is
he"* (Proverbs 23:7).

I could have avoided many pitfalls had I learned
early on that no matter what injustice has been committed
against you, if you allow Him, God can and will turn it all

around for your good and put you in a position to use it to help others. Case in point, the bible talks about Joseph in the book of Genesis. He had the gift of prophecy through dreams. However, he was immature and his gift was undeveloped. His brothers envied him because their father Jacob favored him, but his brothers hated him even more because of his gift. They ended up throwing Joseph into a pit, and later decided to sell him into slavery to avoid killing him. They lied to their father and claimed he was murdered by a wild animal.

Although he ended up as a slave in Egypt, it was not long before he was appointed as overseer of his master's house. While acting as overseer he was falsely accused of attempting to rape his master's wife, and he was sent to prison. But he had favor with God and man, so he prospered even in prison. But, not only did God cause Joseph to prosper wherever he went, but also the people around him and land in which he resided prospered as well. In spite of the public humiliation he was forced to bear, he never surrendered his mind, heart or emotions to his circumstances, because he knew without a doubt that God was always with him. He did not protest his innocence and rebel, but humbled himself and served as a model prisoner. In doing so, he was promoted and became the overseer over the prison. Joseph had the favor of God and an influential anointing that enveloped everyone he came in contact with.

No matter how many times Joseph was victimized, abandoned, falsely accused, and enslaved in some form or another: he continued to forgive and walk in love. Moreover, Joseph never failed to honor the Lord and in return, the Lord never failed to honor him. God always saw fit to make Joseph ruler over those who were supposed to rule over him. Therefore, Joseph was always victorious and prospered in whatever role he played – even in prison. It was his humility, faith, willingness to help others, and God-given gift of prophecy through dream interpretation that was instrumental in leading him out of prison and into his purpose.

Ironically, it was his dreams that appeared to get him in trouble with his family, and sent his life into a downward spiral. But God used the very thing that appeared to be a curse, as a key to unlock purpose and propel him to his destiny. He was eventually promoted from the prison to the palace, and made Governor, second in command over all of Egypt by the Pharaoh himself.

Joseph's painful beginning would fail in comparison to the extraordinary outcome of his journey from the pit to the palace as confirmed in 1 Peter 5:10, *"In his kindness God called you to share in his eternal glory by means of Christ Jesus. So after you have suffered a little while, he will restore, support, and strengthen you, and he will place you on a firm foundation."*

Due to the relationship Joseph and God shared with one another, Joseph never considered questioning God's faithfulness or ability to watch over and protect him. This is because Joseph had never experienced anything contrary. Regardless of how many battles satan raged, God never failed to deliver Joseph. Regardless of what calamity the enemy tried to use to break and kill him, God always turned it around to make and develop Joseph, and in order to save the lives of those around him as he told his brothers in Genesis 50:20, *"You intended to harm me, but God intended it all for good. He brought me to this position so I could save the lives of many people"* (NLT).

Ultimately, God used every one of Joseph's trials to help catapult him higher than anyone, even Joseph himself, could have imagined. God not only used him to save the very brothers that sold him into slavery and abandoned him, but his father and the entire Jewish nation as well. He also used him to save the land of Egypt and many other nations. His very name, Joseph, means savior. He fulfilled his purpose in becoming just that, because He never failed to trust God Whom had not failed to trust him.

Likewise, my children never question my wife's and my ability or faithfulness to provide a home, electricity, heat or running water on a daily basis. This is because they have never experienced otherwise. My children know that my wife and I know they have need of these things and we provide them, so they do not consider doubting our ability to do so. Seeing that my children never experience not having food to eat on a daily basis, wouldn't it be ridiculous for my children to start asking me all day every day, *"Dad, will there be anything for me to eat or drink today?"* or ask, *"Is this my last meal,"* after every meal? There would be no purpose for doubt sense we have always provided for them daily. The same goes for God remaining faithful to us – it will never change.

Joseph did not hold any grudges. He chose to forgive everyone who had hurt and disappointed him. Furthermore, he chose to allow God to mature him and his gift. He also came to understand the purpose and power of his gift through his relationship with God, and never wavered in his confidence. This was a vital requirement for him before taking his position as Egypt's governor. Most of us have probably heard the saying, *"If one does not understand the purpose of a thing, he or she will most likely misuse it."* Fortunately, this was not an issue for Joseph. When his brothers came to Egypt for help, he was not vindictive towards them. Although he tested their character in love, he did not abuse them. When the opportunity came for him to release forgiveness, healing and restoration regarding his brothers and others he did not hesitate. This made it possible for him to be able to release his pain. Yes, Joseph himself released his pain, not God!

Joseph went on to name his eldest son Manasseh, for he said, *"God has made me forget all my troubles and everyone in my father's family"* (Genesis 41:51 NLT). In other words, he was able to fulfill his purpose because he surrendered his pain to God, and the Lord blessed him tremendously as promised in the following scripture, *"So humble yourselves under the mighty power of God, and at the right time he will lift you up in honor. 7) Give all your* worries and cares to God, for he cares about you" (1 Peter 5:6-7 NLT). God not only caused him to forget the pain of his past, but to bless and save the lives of those responsible for it, thus fulfilling his destiny as Joseph – "savior."

My name is Richard meaning *powerful, strong leader, ruler*. Yes, that describes me perfectly and it has nothing to do with what others think, what my wife thinks, or even what I think. It really does not matter what my name or your name is. I may not know you personally, but I can tell you the meaning of your name. Your name means *powerful, strong leader, ruler* as well. Yes, I am sure of it! You can find it in Genesis 1:26-28, "*And God said, Let us make man in our image, after our likeness: and let them have dominion over the fish of the sea, and over the fowl of the air, and over the cattle, and over all the earth, and over every creeping thing that creepeth upon the earth. 27) So God created man in his own image, in the image of God created he him; male and female created he them. 28) And God blessed them, and God said unto them, Be fruitful, and multiply, and replenish the earth, and subdue it: and have dominion over the fish of the sea, and*

over the fowl of the air, and over every living thing that
moveth upon the earth.

It is simply because God clearly defined us before you and I were even created. The meaning of my name Richard describing me as *powerful, strong leader, ruler* is cool and all, but I fully understand that without God's love, guidance, peace, favor, protection and power; I am nothing! Make no mistake, I am only as strong as my relationship with God and my willingness to obey and trust Him. And so with humility and appreciation, I embrace my name and purpose – powerful, strong leader, ruler – Trailblazer!

THE PUPOSE OF PAIN

Over the following decade it would appear as though the prison door would remain a revolving one for me. I had been in and out pretty much for the same things. At that time, my jail stints were a product of my repetitive stinking-thinking and bad decision making. Everything appeared to be happening so fast, a mile-a-minute it seemed. My life was equivalent to a fast moving roller coaster. I lived very fast with too many ups, downs, twists and turns to remember. But I do remember my life spiraling out of control before I could really get a grasp on it or realize to what dangerous extent. I also started using heavier drugs. Yes, I said heavier because this was not my first experience.

I was about twelve years old, and living on the streets when I started smoking cigarettes, and eventually escalated to marijuana around age fourteen. I did not think there was anything wrong with it at the time. I did not feel I acted differently when I smoked marijuana. I considered it calming and "recreational." Well, I had the "rec" part right! It help to wreck my life. I grew more and more dependent on it, as well as increasingly anxious and paranoid. I convinced myself that I needed it often to get me through my "rough days," but to be honest, in the position I was in every day was rough! It also seem to numb me from the pain and pressure I was dealing with.

During my decade of destruction so-to-speak, marijuana diminished in effectiveness for me. Someone suggested I mix it with cocaine in order to revive its effectiveness. There is one thing I have to say about that...mission accomplished! It was as if I opened the very gates of hell in my life. Drugs literally transformed me into a slave. Drugs became to me as Pharaoh was to the Egyptians – a God. Pain and chaos ruled over me like taskmasters. My series of destructive, foolish choices lead me to a path of destruction I could not have ever imagined.

I had just as much access to drugs during my incarceration as I did when I was out in the streets. I convinced myself that I continued to use drugs in jail to cope with my life behind bars. But the truth was, I had failed to end my addiction before I got there. The first time I used drugs, I liked how it made me feel "nothing" and seemed to distance me from my pain and problems. Truth is it gave me a false sense of escape. A sort of *"necessary numbness"* I deemed valuable at that time for a lifestyle such as mine. Each time I used drugs, I was under the illusion that I could reach the same level of euphoria or higher, as I did the very first time I tried it. I later learned that the numbness itself was influenced by a demon and was not constructed to help me shut out pain, but shut out God, whose love would deliver me from my pain, and lead me to my purpose.

Needless to say, there was very little communication with anyone on the outside during this time. A phone call with my grandmother or sister here or there, once or twice a year on a holiday. By this time, I had been alone for so long that I had become accustomed to solitude. Actually, it seemed to work in my favor in such a hostile and chaotic environment as prison. This is because prison is littered with four poisonous ingredients: time, boredom, an idle mind and demonic influence. Once these four things come together, mischief is often inevitable and frequently with deadly consequences. It was about midway through and I had finally reached my "rock bottom" and just wanted to stay out of trouble. But even more so, I wanted out of the pain and torment I had allowed to run my life for as long as I could remember.

There was an inmate everyone referred to as "pastor." He was a born-again believer in Jesus Christ and did not just talk-the-talk, but also walked-the-walk. He spent all day, every day sharing the gospel of Jesus Christ with everyone he came in contact with. He was relentless yet respectful. So, the day had come when I decided to take him up on his offer to attend a daily bible study in which he taught. I remember it now as if it were yesterday.

As he boldly taught the word of God, it was as if each word somehow connected with my spirit and soul. The more I heard; the freer I became. God's word seemed to have a power I had not experienced before. It had an even greater effect on me than drugs, and I did not have to result to anything illegal to obtain it. This would be the day I surrendered my life to Jesus Christ and accepted Him into my heart as my Lord and Savior. It was truly the best decision I have ever made! I did not have to be concerned with being alone anymore. Jesus had come to live inside my heart, and He planned to stay. I believed that this wise decision would bless and change my life during my incarceration. However, I had no idea that God wanted to use me to be a blessing as well. Little did I know; that was only the beginning.

I started attending church consistently. My life changed dramatically. I had found an indescribable, priceless peace as it states in Philippians 4:7, *"And the peace of God, which passeth all understanding, shall keep your hearts and minds through Christ Jesus."* It was at that time I started to understand all the prayers and confessions that my godmother had prayed over my life throughout the years. She planted the seed of Jesus Christ in my life, and now it was being hydrated and nurtured. After service one night, I can remember brushing my hair in the mirror, and hearing the Lord speaking to me, *"You are my Son whom I love. I am here son and I have always been with you. Come closer to me and I will draw nearer to you."* And I heard the spirit of God say, *"Open your bible and read Genesis 1:26. I created you with and for a purpose."* It was at that moment that I truly realized who I was – a purposed-filled son of the King!

Being a "babe-in-Christ" while in incarcerated had its challenges to say the least. I vowed to be positive and stay encouraged, although I was in one of the most negative and discouraging atmospheres known to man. I had always enjoyed reading, and had taken a few college courses prior to going to prison. During my incarceration, I was able to resume taking college courses which was encouraging and helped me to remain hopeful. There were some days I did not consider things so bad, but other days were downright miserable! I surely had my ups and downs, but I would soon learn that happiness in any atmosphere is simply a choice.

God used a particular elderly man to teach me something I would never forget. Whether out in the yard, during mealtimes, church services or recreational time, this guy always seemed to be smiling. He was noticeably peaceful and seemed truly happy. I just could not wrap my head around it. How in the world could this elderly man, or any man for that matter, manage to be consistently happy in a place like this?

One day after church service I struck up a conversation with him. He told me that he was eighty-nine years old and had been in prison for the last thirty-four years, and would most likely die there. He also told me that although he had given his life to Christ just fifteen years prior, that fifteen years was the best years of his eighty-nine-year life. I shared with him how baffled I was as to how he always managed to smile, remain peaceful, and encourage others in the negative, violent, and chaotic atmosphere in which we were trapped in. I wanted to know how he managed to remain content in such a contentious place. The wisdom he shared with me was life changing and continues to bless me to this very day.

He explained how he did not allow his circumstances to dictate his attitude. He went on to say how he had repented of his sins, given his life to Jesus, and was forgiven for all his wrong doings as stated in 1st John

1:9, "*If we confess our sins, He is faithful and just to forgive our sins and cleanse us of all unrighteousness.*" He reiterated that he would probably die in prison, but God had given him a perfect peace within himself and the grace to continue on. He did not consider himself trapped at all. He made it clear that he refused to be sad, down or depressed about his life because to do so would be futile. He then went on to declare who he was – an eighty-nine year old son of God. And it amazed me that even in his old age he continued to embrace and fulfill his purpose.

I was so impressed with his attitude, that it inspired me to practice the same principles as him. Although it was a process and took some time, I and others began to see and experience the fruit of my labor. I also began to understand Isaiah 26:3, "*thou wilt keep him in perfect peace, whose mind is stayed on thee because he trusteth in thee.*" I matured more and more.

The elderly gentleman's testimony was and still remains so powerful to me decades later! It reminds me of a passage from my wife Renda's book, *"Happy Is Me! How to Never Live Unhappy Again!"* It says, "*Living a happy lifestyle does not only change your life for the greater, but can also greatly impact the lives of others around you. I love the story in the bible of the Apostle Paul in Acts 26. Paul was arrested and brought before King Agrippa, where he faced the death penalty for teaching repentance. Normally, when prisoners went before the king, they were not allowed to speak for themselves. Someone would speak and respond to the charges on behalf of the prisoner. However, Paul having the favor of God on his life was allowed to speak directly to the king, governor, and council freely and on his own behalf.*

Paul began by informing the king that he respected him as an expert on such issues, and requested the king be patient so that he could explain the entire matter. Paul proceeded to confirm that he was a Jew, and talked about his childhood and upbringing in relation to studying, following and respecting the teachings of the scribes. He stated how he was much disciplined in those teachings, and suggested that anyone who knew him could substantiate his reputation. As a result, he became a great defender of those teachings. He even began persecuting others for what he felt was their lack of discipline, or for speaking anything he felt was blasphemy or contrary to what he believed to be the truth. However, it all changed one day!

Paul continued on explaining how he had a life changing experience while he was on his way to Damascus; to persecute more Christians.   While on this road, he was blinded by a bright light. It was Jesus Christ of Nazareth asking him, "Why do you persecute Me?" He furthered explained his entire experience to the king. Paul wanted to ensure that the king could relate to what he was trying to reveal to him. He reiterated that the king himself, received the teachings of Moses and the scribes to expect The Christ. Paul begins to break down the attributes of Jesus Whom had blinded him on the road to Damascus. He did this so that the king could identify them as parallel to the attributes of the Christ, whom he was taught to expect.

Paul had hoped the king would be convinced and identify Jesus of Nazareth as the Christ. One cried out to Paul, "You are mad!" He went on to tell Paul that he had indulged himself too much into all that extra teaching, and it was driving Paul insane. But Paul stood his ground and proclaimed he was sane as well as sober! As Paul further addressed the king, he went on to point out the keen discernment and wisdom of the King. We can all agree that Paul himself, having the wisdom of God; knew how to handle that matter wisely. His decision to approach the king with humility and respect was excellent. So much so, that the king himself stated, "You almost persuaded me to become a Christian."

I said all that to get to my main focal point. In the very beginning when King Agrippa informed Paul he was permitted to speak for himself, the first thing Paul said was, "I THINK MYSELF HAPPY" (emphasis added). Wow! Think about that. Paul knew no one else considered his trial as a time to be happy, or a happy situation. However, he was happy because he did not allow his happiness to be determined by an atmosphere or situation. He carried it with him at all times. Like Paul, I do not go anywhere expecting to get happy. I take my happiness with me because it dwells on the inside of me, and it is my lifestyle!"

I love that! Neither the elderly prisoner I had known nor did Paul choose to focus on their painful, bleak, discouraging, hopeless atmosphere. They did not deny that pain was present, yet they decided to concentrate on the grace of God which was sufficient to carry them along their journey, to and through their purpose. Paul said it best in Philippians 4:12-13 as he stated, *"I know how to live on almost nothing or everything. I have learned the secret of living in every situation, whether it is with a full stomach or empty, with plenty or little. 13) For I can do everything through Christ, Who gives me strength"* (NLT).

I encourage you to make the decision to, *"Give all your worries and cares to God, for He cares about you"* (1st Peter 5:7 NLT). You must understand that this scripture has a two-fold meaning. It means that God not only cares about what is happening with you, yet He will also take care of you in spite of it. Therefore, it does not matter who you are, what you have done in your past, or how chaotic your life may seem right now. You too can do as Joseph, the eighty-nine year old elderly gentleman, Paul and I myself, as well as countless others have done. We all took action and surrendered our lives to Christ, despite all the pain we may have suffered at the time. I assure you that although pain may be present in your life, you can make purpose your priority and live the victorious life God intended for you. Now is your time!

NOTES

THE MAKING OF A TRAILBLAZER

CHAPTER 4

FROM MENACE TO MAN

Due to the mercy and favor of God on my life, I was released from prison after serving five years of the five-to-twenty year sentence I was given. Before my release, I had petitioned God to bless me with what I had longed for since I was kid; a close and stable family. My family had been dismantled after my parents' divorce, and I desired for God to fill that void. I then asked God to give me a family of my own. I promised Him I would love and take care of them with all my heart. Faithful as He is, He literally gave me what I had asked for and much more.

It had been about a year after my release, and I was trying to pick-up-the-pieces in my life. For many years I had dreamed of starting my own businesses. I had written my own version of a business plan years prior, so when I was released I followed through on it. In order to support myself, I started my own snow removal business with one shovel and one employee – me! I had no intention on sitting around sulking about who would not give me a job because of my past. I thought, "*Well, there was a time when I was bold enough to be a drug dealer and criminal which cost me everything. So I have everything to gain by starting my own legitimate business. Besides, it does not hurt to try.*" I had looked forward to getting a fresh start and working for myself.

Although shoveling snow was not my dream business, it was a start. I was ecstatic to simply be working, but to have my own business was a major accomplishment for me. As insignificant as a one-shovel-one-man snow removal business may sound to someone else, it was equivalent to a fortune 500 company to me at the time. I never saw it or any business as insignificant or petty. I undoubtingly believe that your business, family, marriage, job, education or anything else in your life, is only as large, or small as you envision it to be. The development, growth and success (or lack thereof) of such things are an expression of your faith.

Although, I would periodically read my bible and attend a church in my neighborhood, I did not join and get connected. Therefore I had no real "root" in the word, or should I say there was no real root of the word in me. Needless to say, I found myself thinking of how I could make more money, much faster. There were two ways in which I had experienced such and both were illegal and dangerous. The two were stealing other's property, and selling drugs.

Well let me start by saying stealing anything was out of the question for me! I wanted nothing else to do with armed robbery, breaking and entering, or anything involving stealing. Although I clearly understood drug dealing was wrong. I more so saw it as a "lesser evil" so-to-speak that would help me get a handle on staying afloat financially and saving some money, which would ultimately keep me from going back to prison. Do you see the irony here? Although bad decisions and committing crimes contributed to me going to jail in the first place, I would use those same two poisons to avoid going back to prison. You may be thinking, *"What in the world were you thinking? Only a fool does that!"* Well, unfortunately I was not the first and will not be the last.

This ridiculous and debilitating way of thinking wreaks havoc in the lives of those bond, as well as free, and does not discriminate when it comes to race, sex, culture, religion or financial ranking. This manner of thinking is self-destructive. Some of you may be saying, *"I don't do that to myself. And most times I can be my own worst critic."* That may even be true, yet, what about when it comes to others? Do you tend to compromise your morals and values in order to flow with popular, less controversial views? If so, James 1:8 defines this kind of person as "double minded" and his or her behavior as "unstable" at all times. Therefore, this kind of person cannot be trusted by anyone – not even himself.

Whenever one tends to justify sin in the lives of others, and view any form of wrong doing as anything other than what it truly is, then it is surely only a matter of time before he or she will also indulge in some form of self-justifying sin in his or her own life. I was obviously in serious need of a mindset and atmosphere adjustment not only to avoid ruining my life, but the lives and families of those who were addicted to the drugs I sold. I know it was God's mercy and grace that covered me at that time. But even then I knew one day that grace would expire if I continued to do as I pleased, and not as I knew what was right. I prayed for God's help – and got it!

FINDING FAVOR

One night while out with a friend, I met a beautiful young lady that caught my attention the moment I laid eyes on her. I introduced myself to her and struck up a conversation. During our chat, I made it a point to be upfront with her. I revealed that I had made some bad choices that resulted in me spending some time in prison. I was relieved at how well she reacted. She was calm and encouraging. She did not hesitate to let me know that she had made some bad choices in her past as well that resulted in painful consequences. Yet, she went on to share how everything changed when she began to trust and follow Jesus Christ, and was now a born-again believer. She was not judgmental and seemed very easy to talk to. She was very confident, but not prideful or arrogant. Even when she divulged that she was a single parent of four daughters, she did not speak shamefully; and rightfully so.

Learning that she had children was not a deterrent for me. She was a single parent working and going to school, yet raising four daughters in the Lord. The fact that she seemed to value her family was impressive to me.

She presented herself very well. It quickly became obvious to me that she loved and respected God, her children, and herself. Talking with her was very encouraging and somewhat soothing. I must admit it was her looks that attracted me to her. But it would ultimately be her encouragement, sense of humor, and commitment to God that would quickly capture my heart, and cause me to fall in love.

For our first date, she invited me to church. This was the first time any woman had ever invited me to church. It was there I saw her brother Aaron. He and I are the same age which is a couple of years older than Renda. As we introduced ourselves to one another, we quickly realized we all had attended the same elementary and middle school together. About eighteen years had passed, so Renda and I initially did not recognize one another. Ironically, I later learned she had once had a huge crush on me when we were kids.

Renda introduced me to her four daughters. When I introduced Renda and her girls to my son Brandon, everyone seemed to get along well. I had never met a woman like Renda before, she never let a conversation end without encouraging me in some way or another. I found myself looking forward to spending time with her and the girls as often as I could. About a month had gone by, when one day I heard God speak to me about Renda and the girls. He said, *"Take care of them and I will bless you."* Hearing that from God was a blessing because I had already fallen in love with her, and the girls stole my heart the day I met them. By this time, Renda also made it clear that she was in love with me as well. I wasted no time asking Renda to marry me, and she said yes. I had also asked for and received her mother's permission to do so.

I must be honest; there were family and friends who were very skeptical about me marrying Renda. They said that I did not know her that well, which was true, but it was mostly because she had children. Some referred to her children as what some call "baggage." But I never once thought of Renda's children as baggage. To me they were little girls with big hearts. And these girls, no different than any other children, needed a loving, active, hands-on father, willfully present in their lives on a consistent basis. I never viewed them as burdens, but blessings and eventually "lifesavers" for me – literally! Despite the naysayers and negative feedback from some, Renda and I were married and proceeded on with optimism. I had finally gotten what I had desired and looked forward to for many years – a family of my own.

Marrying Renda gave me a huge sense of relief. It was the second greatest decision I had ever made, only second to giving my heart to Jesus Christ. I no longer had to be concerned with having a loving wife and family. Renda not only told me she loved me, but showed it as well. More importantly, she loved the Lord. Her unwavering commitment to the Lord and her purpose was attractive to me. She was good for me and to me. I felt blessed to have found her as expressed in Proverbs 18:22, *"Whoso findeth a wife findeth a good thing, and obtaineth favor of the Lord."* Being with her was refreshing to say the least.

Although I was ecstatic about finding my soulmate, there was some concern about making enough money to support and take care of them. I never doubted my capability to make enough money, only how I would do so consistently. Renda was great at encouraging and praying for me. I do not know if she really realizes how much her strong relationship with God influenced me. There were times that I was strengthened simply from listening to her study the word of God and pray. We had our issues as all newlyweds and blended families do, but things seem to be going well.

About six months into our marriage we learned Renda was pregnant. We were both very excited about having a baby together. But as time grew closer for our new baby to arrive, what I then described as reality began to set in. My excitement was overshadowed by fear, which was new for me. With all I had endured and faced as a child, teenager, and in prison, I had never really been fearful. At least not in this way. I began to succumb to fear rather than walk in faith. It is in these times that we should dive deeper into the word of God and prayer. It is in God's word that we find refuge in times of trouble. Fear is not from God. He does not want us to be fearful and confused, and 2nd Timothy 1:7 confirms it. In fact, He gives us power, love, and self-discipline. The proper understanding and execution of these prized possessions are key to help us successfully carry out the role of a trailblazer.

Before now, I had only been responsible for myself. My son was born during the time I was incarcerated so I did not have the long-term, consistent responsibility of being a fulltime parent, and even so after my release. But now, I was not only a fulltime husband, but also a fulltime father of five with a newborn on the way. I began to worry a lot instead of following Proverbs 3:5-6 which instructs us to, *"Trust in the Lord with all your heart; do not depend on your own understanding. 6) Seek his will in all you do, and he will show you which path to take"* (NLT).

I loved my wife and family very much and was committed to staying in my marriage and raising our children together. From the beginning, I made up my mind and heart to never get a divorce, regardless of how tough and challenging things got. I had experienced firsthand the debilitating process and painful residue of divorce, and could not imagine putting my wife and children through that; or myself for that matter. At that time things were starting to get tough.

To add more stress to my already full plate during that time, Renda and I both were taking courses at the University where she worked as the Testing Coordinator. It seemed I was being pressured from all directions. I started worrying more than praying. My faith in God's ability to help me seemed to have dwindled to an all-time low.

I remember satan continuously trying to bombard my thoughts with despair like, "*How are you going to deal with all of this pressure? You aren't used to all this pressure. Doing a little drugs won't hurt. Remember how it used to help you get your mind off everything. You don't have to keep using. Just do it once or twice to help get your mind off all this stuff you have to deal with.*" The enemy offered me poor excuses to surrender to my flesh in which I ultimately accepted. It started with smoking marijuana and escalated to smoking marijuana laced with cocaine. I used it as a crutch and fake escape from pain and pressure. I would try to convince myself that I would only use it occasionally when I felt overwhelmed. I thought I was in control, and not the one being controlled. But that was only an illusion.

Unfortunately, I began to depend more on my own strength, and less on the strength of God. I appeared strong on the outside, but inside I was seeking an exit door. My actions were a prelude to a very dangerous detour from my purpose. At that time, I would have loved to believe that I was only hurting myself and not anyone else. But nothing could be further from the truth. In actuality, I was selfish and only focusing on myself at the time. Not to mention Renda was totally unaware of my past and then present drug use. I had shared with her my experience as a drug dealer, but not as a user. Although I had not used drugs for many years, I was still somewhat ashamed of it. So, I chose not to share that with her. Renda as well as our kids were depending on me to support and be there for them physically, financially, and emotionally; and rightfully so. There was so much at stake. And to add fuel to the fire, I was also risking my freedom. If it were exposed that I was using drugs, I could be hauled off back to jail. Even worse, if I did not stop I could lose everyone and everything I loved, and possibly my own life!

It had been many years since I had used drugs. I had repeatedly dismissed the thoughts and temptation in the past; but not this time. What made this time different? How was the enemy able to successfully infiltrate my thoughts, and influence me to risk it all and disobey God? It is because I let my guard down and he seized the opportunity to strike. How? Well, my previous actions were completely contrary to the following instructions that could have protected me and prevented it all. Ephesians 6:10 instructs us to *"be strong in the Lord and in His mighty power"* (NLT). Notice that it is God's

power that makes us strong and not our own. I stop

trusting and relying on God's strength to sustain me (that

was strike #1). That chapter continues to further instruct

you to *"put on all of God's armor so that you will be able to*

stand firm against the strategies of the devil" (6:11, NLT). I

failed to fully "suit up" which contributed to my instability

and caused me to stumble (this was strike #2). Then it

tells you each protective piece to apply such as the belt of

truth, breastplate of righteousness, shoes of peace,

helmet of salvation, sword of the Spirit, and the shield of

faith. All are important, but even more so faith. This is

because faith is a shield, and its purpose is to prevent the

rest of your armor from taking a direct hit and being

penetrated by the weapons of the enemy. My lack of faith

caused me to suffer direct and consistent attacks that

contributed to me losing my leverage (this was strike #3).

Things seem to spiral out of control quickly. However, the

truth was that I surrendered my control to satan the

moment I *entertained* the thought of using drugs again.

     For one to intentionally hurt and destroy oneself is

to hurt God simultaneously. The bible says in John 10:10,

"The thief cometh not, but for to steal, and to kill, and to

destroy: I am come that they might have life, and that they might have it more abundantly." It is satan who wants to destroy your life, but it is Jesus who came to save it and make it enjoyable. In other words, Jesus not only came to provide a blessed eternal life in heaven, but a purposeful and blessed life here on earth as well. Therefore, when people actively participate in behavior that initiates death instead of life, he or she is not the only one feels the pain. But also Jesus who loved them so much He gave up His own life that they may live.

Proverbs 18:32, *"God arms me with strength, and he makes my way perfect" (NLT).* I cannot stress enough the importance of gleaning your strength and guidance from God. Trailblazers understand that God, and He alone, is their GPS. It is the powerful blood of Jesus that protects and sustains you as you travel through the low valleys of delays and disappointment, as well as climb the steep mountains of success and victory. To follow and submit to God's direction prepares and positions you to lead as well.

As I battled the mind attacks and substance abuse; I was miserable. I had no peace of mind and constantly thought, *"What am I going to do,"* I asked? *"How am I*

going to tell her about everything I am dealing with?"
Well, I had missed the opportunity to do the right thing
and tell her myself, but she found out in such a hurtful way
that I regret to this day.

As a condition of my parole release, I was to make
monthly visits to see my parole officer for the following
two years. I had less than a year to go before the visits
would be complete. During a visit to see my parole officer
I tested positive for drugs. I was immediately taken into
custody and was told I would be going back to prison. I
was encouraged to call my pregnant wife, while she was at
work, and let her know I would not be coming home for a
long time.

I can say without a doubt that was the absolute
hardest thing I ever had to do in my life! Honestly, it was
the first time I had thought of and cared more about
someone else's pain and suffering before my own. When I
called Renda at work and told her, she was speechless for
about ten seconds. She later explained to me that our
brief phone conversation was surreal to her. She stated
she was shocked, confused, devastated, and furious all at
the same time. The guilt, shame, and fear I experienced
when I called Renda is indescribable. It was especially

hard because she was pregnant, I really loved my family, and I did not want my marriage to end. I also knew how she felt about people who struggled with substance abuse. I somewhat remember a conversation Renda and I had several months prior to the revelation of my own personal battle. She had stated to me that she had not dated, nor would not date anyone *who had battled with drug abuse. She made it clear how strongly she felt about it, and could never be with a man who had dealt with that because she did not think anyone could fully recover from that.*"

Renda said she had watched people get hooked on drugs and allow it to destroy them, as well as families, marriages, and even relationships with the Lord. Although she knew the bible said, "What is impossible for man is possible with God," and "I can do all things through Christ which strengthens me," she had never witnessed it first hand when it came to someone she knew getting and staying clean from substance abuse. She knew the problem did not lie with God, and had no doubts that God did not want anyone to live deflated, defeated, and subservient to any tormenting demons. But although she knew Ephesians 6:12 says *"For we are not fighting against flesh-and-blood enemies, but against evil rulers and authorities of the unseen world, against mighty powers in this dark world, and against evil spirits in the heavenly places"* (NLT), she focused on the physical results of their spiritual bondage instead. All she saw was their physical lack of self-respect, uncleanness, and irresponsibility. And so at that time, she did not show them any love and literally had no compassion for them. That is until she found out that the man she had fallen in love with, married, and was carrying his child was indeed himself abusing drugs.

As I sat waiting for the parole officer to determine my fate, I thought about how much pain, disappointment, and embarrassment I had caused Renda, and could only imagine what she must have been going through. Even worse, I had hurt and disappointed God. The emotions I felt at that time were something I had not experienced before. For the first time, my initial thought was not a selfish thought of only myself. My main concern at the time was about my wife and family who I loved very much and wanted to help and not hurt.

I prayed and asked God for His help. I first prayed for Renda and the kids and then myself. I asked God's forgiveness for what I had done and was putting my family through. I also prayed that I would not have to leave my family, and all the responsibility be shifted to Renda without any help to care and provide for everyone. The reality of what I had done had begun to really sink in and torment me. That was one time I remember praying like I had absolutely nothing to lose – because I didn't. The only direction I could go from there was up and I was not settling for anything less. Gravity seemed to be working against me, and the position I was in looked hopeless. In actuality, I had been positioned by God to successfully transition from a menace to a man.

I prayed for God's favor with my parole officer and those making the decision regarding my staying out of prison or not. Again, God extended His mercy and grace and I was sent to a rehabilitation facility instead of back to prison. I stayed for about a month, and shortly after returning home Renda delivered our new baby girl. Although she was a few weeks premature, she was healthy. If ever there was a reason to stay clean, this would have been it. I had already put my family through so much, and wanted to make it up to them. However, those drug demons were not giving up easily. But neither was my "good thing" Renda! When it came to my family, the enemy may have been thinking this would mean the end of our marriage, faith in God, family, purpose and everything else. But to Renda it meant one thing – war!

NOTES

_____

_____

_____

_____

_____

_____

_____

_____

_____

_____

_____

_____

_____

_____

CHAPTER 5

MAN ON FIRE

God said, *"It is not good for the man to be alone. I will make a helper who is just right for him"* (Genesis 2:18, NLT). And for me, her name is Renda! It is one thing for a husband or wife to experience love, unity, and bliss with his or her spouse during the good times in a marriage. But it is altogether phenomenal to experience unconditional love, forgiveness, encouragement, and unwavering support from a spouse during a time of major challenges in a marriage. My wife's love for God, strength, resilience, faith, relentless optimism, and willingness to go after whatever she set her heart and mind towards, is what made me want to spend the rest of my life with her. It was those same attributes she embodied, that would also compel her to stay in our marriage, in spite of all the criticism and backlash from others, in addition to, standing against her own fear and doubt.

I remember one day when I came home high as a kite and defiant. Instead of fighting with me, she chose to fight for me. She fearlessly looked me straight in the eyes, and spoke with authority to the demonic spirits oppressing me. She stated that God had given her authority over demons and not the other way around. She went on to say how I, nor our family, did not belong to satan and was not subject to any demonic spirits or curses. She also said that our home was where the Holy Spirit lived, and where the Spirit of the Lord is; there is freedom from oppression. She concluded by binding the spirits in the name of Jesus and commanding them to leave.

I tried to act as though her words meant nothing, but truthfully it scared me pretty badly, and blew my high so I left. When I returned about an hour later, Renda along with others, were in our living room interceding for me. As I entered the house and headed straight down the hall toward our bedroom I heard, "*Hi Richard. We are praying for you.*" No derogatory or demeaning remarks, and no aggression. I had never experienced anything like that before, and could not wrap my head around it. These people came out in the middle of the night to pray for me and my family in our own home. Some of you may be thinking the way in which I did at the time, "*Who does that?*" The answer would be – trailblazers!

I had battled the addiction off and on for about five or six months. By that time my disobedience and excuses had run their course. Some of the people who had been praying for me were now praying for Renda to leave me. She was told that I would only drag her and the kids down with me. Renda was advised to leave me immediately, and given the option for her and the kids to live with a family member until she could get back on her feet. She was encouraged to consider my past incarceration and battle with addiction at that time, and accept that it was impossible for me to change. I completely understand that those people were not telling her these things because they wanted to see her marriage end, or to cause her more grief. Those were people who loved and cared about her and our children, and wanted to see them joyful and safe. Therefore, I was not angry or resentful toward them for advising Renda in the way in which they did. If it were my loved one being subjected to that type of treatment, I have no doubt that I would have felt and reacted the same way at that time – most likely worse.

One day I seriously injured my hand and ended up in the Emergency Room, and ultimately surgery. I was in a lot of mental, emotional, and now physical pain as well. I could not do anything with my post-surgical limb and felt completely helpless. I had no strength of my own and had to totally depend on God. The moment of my true humbling had finally come. You see, most people, especially those with an addiction, make the mistake of confusing God's patience with acceptance or ignorance. To them, when God does not allow anything drastic or life-threatening to occur in their life for a lengthy period of time, people assume they have successfully managed to hide "under the radar," and that God is not aware of what they continuously do. They become master manipulators, who believe their own lies. But don't get it misconstrued! As Galatians 6:7 says, *"Be not deceived: God is not mocked: for whatsoever a man soweth, that shall he also reap."*

I cried out to God and poured my heart out and asked Him to help me. I also vowed to never touch drugs again. That was the day in which I was truly ready to submit to God and receive His deliverance from the bondage of that addiction. I was ready and willing to transition into the husband, father, and over all man of God He created and predestined me to be.

Meanwhile, Renda was experiencing relentless attacks from what appeared to be all directions and was feeling overwhelmed. She had left with the kids and had been staying with a relative for a few days when I injured myself. When she came to the hospital I apologized for everything I had put our family through. I shared with her how I had surrendered to the Lord and that I was done with using drugs. I told her how much I missed her and the kids and really wanted my family back. In addition, I knew I would be unable to take care of myself for eight weeks due to the surgery and rehabilitation of my hand, and I needed her help. Renda reluctantly agreed to stay with me.

About a week or so after my surgery, the pain was not constricted to my hand alone, but engulfed my entire limb. The pain was awful as well as my attitude. I had managed to paint a picture of myself as a victim in indescribable pain who should be comforted. I was so full of myself and selfish. I had quickly forgotten all about the pain, disappointment, and shame I had caused everyone else for the last six months. Renda had surpassed hurt and shifted to full blown anger. During a brief phone conversation one morning with a loved one, she was reminded of how foolish and ridiculous she looked to others for staying in the marriage and helping me during my post-surgical rehabilitation and my detoxing. She was told that I would only end up using drugs again, and she was strongly encouraged to get out of the marriage as soon as possible. It had become apparent at that time that my wife was virtually at her wits end and ready to leave me for good.

However, Renda shared a conversation with me that she had with God that morning that changed everything. She said God told her not to leave me, so she asked, "*Lord, why should I stay? You know everything he has put us through, and how foolish I look to people. I don't want to deal with it anymore. Lord, why should I believe him? Why would this time be any different?*" The Lord then asked her, "*Are those people your God, or am I your God?*" She replied, "*Lord, You are my God.*" The Lord went on to say, "*The problem isn't your believing other people, or even Richard. It is your failure to believe Me. You believe in Me, but that isn't the same as **believing Me**. You must go further and activate your faith. I want you to stay with Richard; but give him to me. If you do what I tell you to do, I promise you that I will remove the desire and appetite for drugs from him and he will not touch it again. If you pay **no** attention to what others think, and do as I* *say; I will bless your family more than you could ever imagine."* She responded, *"Yes Lord, I will,"* as a fountain of tears streamed down her face. Renda said God then instructed her to create an atmosphere of praise by playing worship CDs over, and over, and over again; as often as possible. She was also told to encourage me, and to never use my past as leverage to attack, retaliate, or manipulate me.

It was at that moment that Renda made the decision to transition from believing in God to literally believing God without doubting, in spite of how foolish she appeared to others and even herself. In other words, she doubted her own doubt! Her sacrificial decision to accept and activate her role as an individual vehicle for God's purpose for my life, in conjunction with hers, annihilated generational curses and positioned our family to live victorious in every area of our lives. I can honestly say Renda has never used my past against me, even to this day. I am so fortunate to have the God-loving, wonderful wife that I have. I cannot thank her enough for her willingness to long-suffer with me, and allow God to express His unconditional love, forgiveness, mercy, grace, strength, and help through her during that time. It was

God, my wife, and my kids that encouraged me and kept me going despite being at my lowest point. Words cannot express my gratitude for the Lord and his priceless gift of Jesus Christ.

Neither Renda nor I could have imagined how quickly God would take us from despair in the morning to hope and gladness by the afternoon and fulfill Isaiah 61: 3, *"To appoint unto them that mourn in Zion, to give unto them beauty for ashes, the oil of joy for mourning, the garment of praise for the spirit of heaviness; that they might be called trees of righteousness, the planting of the Lord, that he might be glorified."* I am so humbled and thankful to God for His faithfulness! That day I was freed from that addiction without a twelve step program and have remained so ever since. It has been fifteen years and counting!

Do not misunderstand me. I have nothing against rehab treatments like twelve step programs, but I needed much more than that. I needed the power-filled word and direction from the Lord that would change my life forever. When Christ died on the cross for our sins, he paid the price so that no one has to remain in bondage. Some substance abuse rehab programs influence you to believe that "once an addict, always an addict." According to the word of God that is inaccurate. Jesus Himself has the correct and final say regarding deliverance and freedom from any sin, *"If the Son therefore shall make you free, ye shall be free indeed"* (John 8:36). It is vital that we receive and activate what God says about us instead of what people tend to say about us; regardless of their good intentions. Despite the labels the enemy tries to brand you with, you are who and what God says you are – His righteous. Romans 4:5 says, *"But people are counted as righteous, not because of their work, but because of their faith in God who forgives sinners.*

LEARNING TO LEAD

Adam and Eve were created in God's image and given all authority to lead the earth in producing and reproducing God's reflection of authority in Heaven; here in the earth. However, Genesis chapter 3 gives us a snapshot of how the enemy persuaded Eve to renounce her God-given authority. Not only did she and Adam both surrender their authority by way of doubt and unbelief, but also simultaneously transferred it to the enemy in the process. And believe it or not, satan is still using that same method of operation to continue deceiving many others out of their inherited power and leadership position. Many of you may be asking, "*Jesus shed His blood, died for our sins, rose from the grave, and relinquished man's authority and leadership position in the earth, so how in the world is satan still able to get away with it?*" Well, let me explain.

The enemy understands something that many human beings do not, or simply continue to take for granted. First of all, God is the principal source of authority. From the beginning, all authority was created and disbursed by Him. So, when satan was kicked out of Heaven, he was stripped of his leadership position and authority he once held as angelic worship leader; before coming to the earth. Secondly, satan knew and understood that God is the author and supplier of authority, and there was no way he would be able to regain it again. He also knew that he was not capable of creating it. This is because he is an imitator; not an originator!

There is one other thing the enemy was well aware of, which also played a pivotal role, as to why he has continued to gain the upper hand on many people. He understood what I call a *law of authority*. Like energy, God's 'delegated' authority cannot be created or destroyed; but it can be transferred. For that reason, he did not waste time trying to kill, steal, or destroy Eve's authority. He simply convinced her to willingly transfer it to him. Unfortunately, many today are still listening to satan's lies and repeating the same mistake as Eve. His goal is to cause you to doubt and not believe God's word that you were created by God, in His image, as a powerful righteous leader with great influence.

When you give your heart to Jesus Christ and trust and obey Him; you accept God's righteousness. And with God's righteousness comes His reinstated authority. Furthermore, once that reinstated authority is accepted, it is everyone's responsibility to get understanding of it; and put it to use. I know this, satan knows this, and I want to make sure you know it as well. Not only does the enemy know this, but hates that there is absolutely nothing he can do about it because his ability is very limited, as well as subject to all God's delegated authority. But that will not stop the enemy from trying to persuade you to self-destruct by renouncing your reinstated God-given authority. How? The same way in which he has always done so – through doubt and unbelief.

If He can get you to doubt and not believe God's word, reject God's righteousness, and live your life as a victim; his mission would be accomplished by way of your surrendering to him without a struggle. God's gift of a sweat-less victory was given to man; not satan. So I encourage you to confess and repent of your sins, give your heart to Jesus, receive God's righteousness and reinstated authority, and give the enemy what belongs to him – a great, big gift of nothing!

SAME POISON, DIFFERENT PACKAGE – RETURNED TO SENDER

It was about two months after I was delivered from the bondage of substance abuse that we learned Renda was pregnant again. Our youngest was only five months old at the time. Most people probably thought that I would be frantic and regress back to my former self-destructive actions; but nope! I am pretty sure satan thought that the news would surely devastate and break me for good, but it did not. Neither did I feel sorry for myself. There was no time or place for pity. I had to man-up and take care of my family. Besides, I had to support and encourage my wife. For her, the news of being pregnant again while nursing a five-month-old, and potty-training a two-year-old at the time, did not go over so well early on!

Hearing my wife was pregnant again did not at all weaken me; but in some way managed to strengthen me. Somehow, the news seemed to ignite a new level of responsibility and hope in me. I enveloped myself in the word of God, and I seemed to grow a little stronger day by day. Don't get me wrong. It was a challenging and lengthy process, but not impossible. In fact, it proved to be very well worth it. I began to lean more on God and less on myself. The bible says in Proverbs 4:7, "*Wisdom is the principal thing; therefore get wisdom: and with all thy getting get understanding.*" Yet, in order to obtain wisdom, one must go to God as stated in the following scripture, "*If you need wisdom, ask our generous God, and he will give it to you. He will not rebuke you for asking*" (NLT). And when I asked God for His wisdom and guidance concerning my life, He did not hesitate to teach me.

I learned that the substance abuse was the outward expression of my inward problems, but not the root. The root of my problems was doubt and unbelief in God's word. There were several times after my deliverance in which the enemy tried to convince me that I was never really delivered and free from the fear and bondage of substance abuse. But I had firmly grabbed hold of 2nd Timothy 1:7, *"For God has not given us a spirit of fear and timidity but of power, love and self-discipline"* (NLT). As a result, the choice was up to me to maintain my deliverance and freedom.

It was my responsibility to trust God, stand on His word, and continue to grow and mature in the things of God. I understood that I was not the only person satan hated and wanted to destroy. I had to believe and know that God had delivered and consecrated me unto himself and planned to keep it that way. Any plans that the enemy had to tempt and overtake me, God had already provided me with the wisdom and weapons to be victorious every time as stated in 1st Corinthians 10:13, *"The temptations in your life are no different from what others experience. And God is faithful. He will not allow the temptation to be more than you can stand. When you are* tempted, he will show you a way out so that you can endure" (NLT).

If you or someone you know is facing obstacles that appear bigger than God; know that it is only an illusion. Regardless of how others may laugh-you-to-scorn for believing God for a miracle; don't give up! Make it a habit to doubt any doubt that tries to diminish your faith in God's word. There are times that you will have to do as David did and encourage yourself in the Lord (1st Samuel 30:6). No matter how impossible a situation looks, know that with God nothing is impossible (Luke 1:27). Keep the faith and move forward!

KEEP YOUR EYES ON THE PRIZE

In Philippians 3:13-14, Paul, a trailblazer himself, encourages other trailblazers to forget the past. He urges us to press forward and focus on what lies ahead. He then singles out the importance of completing the course God has placed in front of each of us, in order to receive the heavenly prize God is calling us to through Jesus Christ. In other words, focus on what is important to God because He is always focused on what is important to you.

My family was now my first priority. During my wife's pregnancy with our seventh child, it appeared she spent more time in the hospital than at home. It was a very challenging pregnancy for us from beginning to end, but we held on to the word of God. In fact, my wife went into preterm labor while teaching bible study at the church we'd belonged to at that time. Funny thing is, she did not tell anyone she was in labor until she had finished the lesson. She then spent the next forty and a half hours in labor. Ironically, she said that despite her sixth labor being the longest, it was the best labor she had ever experienced. She explained that although her sixth labor had lasted far longer than her five previous labors, she had now learned the true purpose of her labor pain and was now able to embrace God's peace during the experience. Yes, the pain of childbirth had remained the same, but her perspective of that pain had minimized its effects. And one thing remained for sure, this pain was not unto death, but to bring forth life. This revelation of pain not only changed my perspective – but my life as well.

THE PURPOSE OF PAIN

Becoming a trailblazer is not an easy task. There is a transition, a development of sort that must take place. In the early stage, trials of ridicule, discouragement, betrayal, jealousy, false accusations, rejection, alienation, deliberate sabotage, and character assassinations are measly attempts to distract you. I must warn you that it may hurt – a lot! However, once you understand the purpose of pain and the revelation of its intent; you can minimize its effects and do not have to be destroyed by it.

Now, I must dig a little deeper into the subject of pain, and how its intent depends on the sender and the receiver. The sender's pain may be for debilitating, diabolical, and deadly purposes. For example, Joseph's brothers throwing him into a pit, and selling him into slavery. However, the sender's pain may be for reconstructive, life-sustaining purposes. For example, Moses sister Miriam being struck with leprosy for seven days after angering the Lord by gossiping about Moses with their brother Aaron. Although she suffered great pain, it was temporal and for redemptive purposes.

Let us start with two definitions of pain. I will call them pain #1 and pain #2, and then I will follow up with God's original purpose of man's pain.

- Pain #1 – punishment (it is the word *Lupe'* in the Greek meaning - *grief, affliction*. It is physical, mental, or emotional in regard to penalty and retribution.)

- Pain #2 – trouble, care, or effort taken to accomplish something (it can be an indicator or sign that some sort of action will be taken to accomplish something.)

Let us look at Genesis 3:16. The woman's consequence for sin was physical and emotional pain (pain #1). Then in Genesis 3:17, Adam too is cursed with the pain of (physical) labor (pain #1) as punishment for his sin. Both their futures looked hopeless. But God is a God of hope. Even when we mess up and have to endure painful consequences, we are not hopeless.

God, the sender of the man and woman's pain, had a two-fold intention for it. It was punishment, to accomplish something – redemption. Romans 6:23 says, *"For the wages of sin is death; but the gift of God is eternal life through Jesus Christ our Lord."* Take note that it is not pain, but sin that definitely leads to (physical and/or spiritual) death. But even when it comes to sin, God has made a way of escaping (eternal) death by way of redemption through Jesus Christ. Neither sin nor pain have to lead to death. In other words, death as a result of sin or pain can be optional, and contingent upon one's choices.

God never intended for man's pain to be permanent and lead to death; only temporal and lead to life. It is in Genesis 3:15 where God actually gives them the victory over their pain before He even punishes them with it. He informed them of the fact that the enemy and his seed (demons) would cause the woman and her seed (Jesus Christ) pain, yet the enemy would be subject to Jesus. And it is through Christ's victory that satan is also subject to God's righteous. So according to Romans 8:2, God does not have (eternal) death waiting for us; but eternal life through Christ; by which we too are victorious.

It is in Genesis 16:13 that God's descriptive name of *"EL ROI"* is mentioned. It translates as *"the God who sees me."* This name was given by Hagar the mother of Ishmael, Abraham's eldest son, to describe God during a very painful time in her life. Although she was suffering anguish and felt no one cared about her and what she was going through, God confirmed that he could not only see her present pain, but also her future victory in fulfilling her purpose. Despite satan's purpose for Hagar's pain, God had a greater plan. It was during her pain that she was willing to humble herself, trust God, and receive the revelation of how much He loved her and remained in control.

The Lord is not ignorant of satan's schemes, and knows the enemy's purpose for pain is always diabolical, debilitating, and purposed to result in (physical and spiritual) death. The enemy's purpose for pain never changes. And so, it is up to the receiver to reject its original purpose and use his or her God-given authority to force it to conform to the result that is favorable for the receiver. God does not want us to live our lives as victims and hostages of the enemy's pain. For that reason, you know that the pain the enemy may unleash for your destruction, God can turn around for your good.

God's curse for the woman's sin was for her to experience pain during childbirth, yet, it was not His intention for that pain to kill her. In fact, Mary, the mother or Jesus, brought forth the Savior of the world in pain that was not only unto human life, but eternal life for all to receive. Take note that Jesus Himself suffered pain from the enemy. Yet, although the pain satan unleashed on Jesus was unequivocally purposed for (physical and spiritual) death and hell, it was Jesus' rejection of its original purpose, and use of His authority to overcome death, hell, and the grave; that resulted in a favorable outcome for man as well as Christ.

The bible says in Philippians 4:6-7, *"Don't worry about anything; instead, pray about everything. Tell God what you need, and thank him for all he has done. 7) Then you will experience God's peace, which exceeds anything we can understand. His peace will guard your hearts and minds as you live in Christ Jesus."* My wife's possession of God's peace during her labor was validated when the doctor and nurses all came running into the room in what seemed to be a panic. It was said that the baby was in distress, and her heart rate had dropped significantly.   We were told that Renda would have to deliver our baby as quickly as possible or she may not make it. It was as if Renda did not here a word they said. She did not fret or panic, but remained calm. Prayer had already gone forth and we continued to stand on the word of God regarding both Renda and our baby, "*I shall not die, but live, and declare the works of the Lord*" (Psalms 118:17). I was so grateful to God for my wife and the baby coming through labor healthy, and in God's perfect peace.

I must say that little by little, Renda's peace began to infect me as well. It was exactly what I needed. I had buried the past and could now focus on my family. It had been during the birth of our daughter Rachel, and throughout our pregnancy with Ri'Char that my mother and I really began to "mend fences" and reestablish our relationship. I had been in contact with my siblings and parents for a while, but it did not seem much had changed. However, the past was just that – the past. I had let go of all the hurt, pain, and unforgiveness that had steered me in the wrong direction in times past. I was in a good place in my life. God had forgiven me, and I had forgiven my parents and everyone else I felt had hurt or disappointed me in some way. God had set me free and I had followed suit. And it was a good thing that I did. I had no idea how my allowing God to change me, would bless me, my family, and others in ways I never could have imagined.

I not only thank God for rescuing me from my pain, but also for loving me during my madness. He continues by helping me to use my testimony to help others. His love for me has been prevalent and continues so to this day. There are many ways in which He chooses to express His love to me; one of which being through my family and wife. It was my wife's love and forgiveness towards me that helped save my life. But it was her willingness to cover me with prayer, encouragement, and respect that helped to catapult me, and set the stage for God to transform me from a Hell-raiser into a Trailblazer, to execute what I was called by God to do – ignite the nations!

NOTES

_____

_____

_____

_____

_____

_____

_____

_____

_____

_____

_____

_____

_____

_____

CHAPTER 6

IGNITE THE NATIONS

LOVE TEST

Imagine you are required to take a mandatory test just before your death which would determine where you spend eternity. The test would be given by God Himself ⋯at there is no way possible for anyone to cheat. Imagine that upon your birth, God hands you a non-erasable pen and a checkbook. It appears to be endless "agape love" (unconditional love) checks inside, for you to write as often as you like. He instructs you to keep an accurate and consistent record of every check you right and to whom you write it to. He also wants the coded as follows: F-family, FR-friend, E-enemy, S-stranger, P-prisoner and SK-sick. God is sure to stress to you that your check writing days are numbered, however, he doesn't tell you the exact number of days you have until your check writing days are complete.

The day has finally come when you must give an account of the "love" checkbooks God gave you at your birth. Let's say you wrote three billion love checks to F-

family, one billion to FR-friends, five thousand to Enemies, fifty to S-strangers, and none to P-prisoners or SK-sick I imagine the story could go something like this- God says, "well, son/daughter, I see you have written billions of love checks to your family, but most read 'stop payment' when you got angry with them. You wrote three billion to friends, but 2,900,900,000 must be subtracted, because those checks were written with ulterior motives in your heart and aren't worth anything. Five thousand you wrote to those you considered your enemies, but forty-five hundred out that five thousand were written to family, in which most bounced! Fifty love checks were written to strangers during the holiday season, only for the purpose of a tax write-off. Finally, you wrote no love checks to any physical or spiritual prisoners, or the sick because you felt they didn't deserve any! You also complained about not having enough time to do all that I instructed you to do, but when you were laid off of your job, you made making money your top priority. You didn't trust me with your life, so why trust me with your death? First Corinthians 13:1-8 says that in spite of operating in various spiritual gifts, without love, we profit nothing. Love never fails! Although this story is fictional, the reality is that there really is a love test

(Mt. 25:31-46). The only way to pass successfully, is to study and obey God's word by his standards and not man's. Follow your study guide (the Bible) and you'll pass without a doubt! Here are some reference scriptures on how to treat others: family- 1 John 4:20-21, friends-Prov. 18:24, enemies- Mt. 5:44-45, strangers-Heb. 13:2, prisoners and sick -Mt. 25:36. Copyright © 2003, Renda Horne

My wife Renda is a writer and author among the many hats she wears. The *"The Love Test"* is one of my favorite short stories of hers. For me, it embodies the identity of who God is as well as what He represents. It is also the foundation of the path in which Jesus paved for us all to go and ignite the nations of the world with the gospel of Jesus Christ. It is the totality and expression of the two greatest commandments which support, as well as fulfill, the Ten Commandments – LOVE! Romans 13:10 confirms it, *"Love does no wrong to others, so love fulfills the requirements of the law"* (NLT).

Trailblazers freely receive God's love, as well as freely share it. This is because they know and understand that His unconditional love is what drew them to Christ, and it is that same magnetic love manifest in and through us that draws others to Christ (1st John 4:19). It truly takes God's love and strength to operate in such a blessed position as a trailblazer. And keep in mind it is that same love, along with the word of God, wisdom, endurance, obedience and a matured character; that will help you remain there.

A trailblazer recognizes that his or her path is established by God's word and love; not man's. We also understand that people waver in their feelings and words, but God does not. There have been some people who have encouraged me one day, only to speak words of discouragement the next. So, I do not waste time trying to please man. Like Christ, I aim to please God. In addition, I trust Him to continue to protect, direct, and correct me such as noted in Philippians 1:6, *"And I am certain that God, who began the good work within you will continue his work until it is finally finished on the day when Christ Jesus returns"* (NLT). I want my desires to line up with God's desires. I want God to use me, and I give him permission to do so. I not only give Him full permission to think through my mind, speak through my mouth, and move through my body; but to also love through my heart.

LOVE IS...

It seemed that life had come full circle for my mother's and my relationship. She and I both had spent a few months working on bridging the gap between us by talking and spending more time together. The both of us had left the past behind us and seemed to be moving forward. I am glad to say we made a lot of progress. The fact that I had my ways, and my mother could be very difficult to please at times would be challenging; but we managed to work it out. She did appear more humbled than she was when I was a kid. But she remained very blunt and forthcoming with her feelings and opinions, and did not hold back when expressing them. But none of that mattered at the time. Truth is, despite everything – I loved her, and often looked forward to seeing her. It was obvious that God was doing exactly what I wanted Him to do. He was teaching me what real love is; and how to execute it as stated in 1st Corinthians 13:4-7, "*Love is patient and kind. Love is not jealous or boastful or proud 5) or rude. It does not demand its own way. It is not irritable, and it keeps no record of being wronged. 6) It does not rejoice about injustice but rejoices whenever the truth wins out. 7) Love never gives up, never loses faith, is always hopeful and endures through every circumstance"* (NLT).

Although I loved my family, there was a time when I was so busy working and trying to take care of them, that I hardly spent any quality time with them – especially on the weekends. So, one weekend day in particular, I planned and looked forward to spending some time with my wife and kids. But to my surprise, my wife said she would be too busy that day to do so. Although her reaction to my plans seemed strange, I did not protest. Turns out, my wife had secretly spent part of that day with my mother. My mother had asked Renda if it were okay for her and one of my sisters to plan a surprise dinner for me to celebrate my upcoming birthday. Renda was not only okay with it, but offered to help as well. My mother and sister did a great job, and I really enjoyed my birthday dinner. It was special to me. I just did not realize how special that time we spent together would turn out to be.

My mother would not complain of not feeling well to me, but Renda noticed and mentioned to me how tired and depleted my mother appeared over a few months period. Although my mother had been in the hospital a couple of times, she was not completely truthful regarding her diagnosis, and down played the seriousness of it. My wife and I visited her in the hospital and enjoyed the time with her. During my wife's "solo" visits with my mother, they would have what she called heart-to-heart talks. My mother shared feelings with my wife that I never knew she had. She talked about how guilty she felt for the way in which she lived her life, how she had failed as a mother, and for the pain she believed she had caused my siblings and me.

Renda shared the gospel with her and told her that she did not have to carry all that guilt, shame, and heaviness. She encouraged her to repent and give her heart and all of burdens to Jesus because He loved her and wanted to change her life. But she seemed to be stuck in the guilt of her past. Renda said it was as if my mother felt she deserved to bare those things because of all the mistakes she had made in her life.

She tried to reassure her that God is not a God of the past, but of the present and future. Renda also told her how God sent His Son Jesus to die on the cross for her sins, and that He raised Him from the dead; because He wanted to give her a new beginning. She reiterated to my mother the fact that I had forgiven my mother long ago.

She told my mother how important it was for her to not only forgive herself, but to ask for God's forgiveness as well, as instructed in 1st John 1:9, *"If we confess our sins, he is faithful and just to forgive our sins and to cleanse us from all unrighteousness."* Although my mother listened as if she were a child listening to a teacher, at that time she could not see herself as worthy of God's gift. Renda and I both continued praying for and with her, during, and in between her hospital stays.

It was not long after my mother had been released from one hospital that she was admitted into another hospital. When we received the call that my mother was back in the hospital, we went to see her. Once again, she appeared to be okay to me. She was alert, talking, and even joking with family, friends, and the hospital staff at times. I, as well as other family members, would go and sit with her for hours at a time. One day in particular, I told her I would be back later that evening to spend the night with her, but got busy and did not make it back. I knew my wife and mother-in-law were going to visit her that evening, so I did not feel so bad about not making it back myself.

My mother really liked my mother-in-law, and asked Renda if she would bring her when she came to visit that evening. My mother-in-law liked my mother and looked forward to the visit. Renda told me how she and my mother-in-law, along with my aunt and uncle had all enjoyed visiting with my mother and one another.

Renda stated that before leaving, she hugged my mother and told her she loved her. She also reassured her that we would call her that same evening, and we would be back early the next morning. When Renda got home, we tried calling her, but she did not answer. I assumed she was asleep and did not want to disturb her. This somewhat put my mind at peace. But it would be short lived. Early the next morning, we received the news that my mother was unresponsive and they were unable to wake her. She never regained consciousness and ultimately passed away.

I felt like I had been run over by a truck! All I could think about was how things could have been different if only I had stayed the night with her like I first planned. Guilt ate at me. Not only because I did not stay the night with her, but also because I felt I should have To be honest, I wasn't aware of her repenting and giving her life I later thought about a statement she had made a month prior after Renda asked her if she was feeling okay. She replied, *"I'm okay and I'm determined to live long enough to give my son this dinner for his birthday."* I thought to myself, *"She probably knew she was going to pass away, and was indirectly letting us know. But I was too busy to spend her last night alive with her."*

It is never wise to take your life, or anyone else's life for granted. People can be here today, but gone tomorrow. Apologies and "I love you" are great when speaking to someone while they are still alive, but it is null, void, and useless after they have passed away. This is why it is so important to forgive and move forward with life while your loved ones are alive.

Although I had forgiven my mother, and told her I loved her countless times before her death; God only knows how much I miss her! I would easily give my right arm if I could just spend thirty seconds with her again. Believe me, if I knew then what I know now, the last night she spent on this earth would have been much different. I would have never separated from her that day! I would have laid beside her and held her in my arms, while constantly praying for her and repeating, *"Mama, I love you so much,"* until she took her last breath! Her death forever changed my life.

Once I let go of the guilt and went through the grieving process, I went into a sort of "what if" way of thinking when it came to my mother. I thought of how much my mother and I both enjoyed revitalizing our relationship, and how nicely things could have developed had she not passed away. I thought of how excited we both were when she planned and hosted my birthday dinner, and how great it would have been for me to honor her for her birthday that upcoming fall. I also thought of how she visited with Renda during Renda's hospital admission for pregnancy complications, as well as when our two youngest children were born. I imagined how great it would have been for her to be alive to see my children grow up, and watch me evolve as a husband and father. We were really getting close; but then she passed away. In all honesty, I felt cheated and could not understand why I was not granted more time with her. Yet, I took comfort in God's word, *"Trust in the Lord with all thine heart; do not depend on your own understanding"* (Proverbs 3:5, NLT). No matter how bewildering a situation may appear, one should take solace in the fact that God loves us and is always in control.

FROM TRAGEDY TO TRIUMPH

It was after my mother's death when I really started to reevaluate my priorities and inquire about my purpose. Although I had not pinpointed my specific, individual purpose at that time; I knew it would somehow involve my kids and kids in general. As the months and years went by, I thought more and more of not only my own purpose, but more so of my children's purpose.

I really enjoyed spending time with them and learning what they were interested in. It was often during vacations that I could almost pinpoint what they enjoyed and were most passionate about doing, because it was the first thing they would navigate towards. I made it my top priority to teach, encourage, and reassure them that they were talented children of God, which meant that they could achieve anything. I was proactive in doing so because I understood all too well what potential pitfalls await a child who lacks the personal grooming, guidance, and quality time of his or her parents.

I enjoyed being a husband and I was appreciative of the wife I had been blessed with, and we enjoyed spending time together. It seemed everyone recognized how much I loved and enjoyed spending time with my family. Yet, in addition, the highlight of my life was being a father. I did not consider my kids as burdens; but blessings. It was truly rewarding for me to consistently take them to church, visit them at school, go with them on field trips, take them to parades, take them fishing, help them talk their mom into letting them have a dog, help them with projects, teach them how to swim, and simply be there to protect them in the process.

Plain and simple, it is nothing less than fulfilling for me to be given the opportunity to do with my kids the very things I had longed for my parents, or a mentor to do with me when I was a kid. In hind sight, it all boiled down to two words for a kid like me – love and care. So, I became passionate about annihilating those pitfalls as an option for my children, and to create an avenue for them to soar. There are plenty of lessons I was prepared to teach my children. But ironically, I was not at all prepared for the revelation my Father God would disclose to me through my children – my purpose!

Our kids were all set to perform in a talent show competition hosted by the church we belonged to at the time. The children performing appeared excited, and appeared to be having a good time. A part of their excitement may have been due to the opportunity to be declared as the winner and ultimately receive a cash prize. In spite of the fact that there would only be one winner, I anticipated that it would be a really fun way to encourage and envelope the children for the glory of God – which it did.

God has given me a heart for children, and I believe it is vital to involve them in exciting, encouraging, creative, and fun activities that will help them recognize, unlock, and ignite the vision and purpose on the inside of them. More importantly, I believe that as born-again believing adults and leaders, we must teach kids that their talents are God's gift and should be used to glorify Him – and Him alone. To successfully do that, we must lead by example and understand that our actions, as well as reactions, are pivotal as to how our children perceive what is pleasing or displeasing to God. So, when trailblazers make a commitment to understand, trust, and obey God's word and respect it as supreme, we are simultaneously paving a path for children to successfully do the same as advised in Proverbs 22:6 states, *"Direct your children onto the right path, and when they are older, they will not leave it"* (NLT).

Although I really enjoyed the church's talent show competition, I could not help but imagine how much more productive, encouraging, and inspiring a youth talent show could be if it were not a competition. I imagined how great it would be to host a youth talent showcase based on teamwork instead of competition. There would be no individual winner, no individual recognition, and no cash prize offered. It would be a talent showcase in which the children perform with the purpose of honoring God with the very talents and gifts He blessed them with. It would be the ultimate tribute to our Lord and King. The goal of the performers would ultimately be to glorify God. God Himself would receive all the glory, honor, and praise by way of His children and all those involved. As a result, the children could reap awesome benefits such as: becoming a trailblazer, teamwork, discovering one's purpose, spiritual direction, encouraging others and receiving encouragement, increasing self-esteem, the revelation of new or more talents and gifts, an opportunity to share the gospel, self-confidence, receiving and giving support, spiritual development and maturity, creativity, meeting new friends, and impacting the world for the glory of God. Most importantly, they will receive the love and blessings of God.

Now let me make it clear that I do not think that all competition is bad or unhealthy. Neither do I believe that there was any malicious intent for anyone performing to be hurt or disappointed by not winning at the church's talent competition. Still, children often tend to see things in black or white. Oftentimes when it comes to kids, anyone that is not openly recognized or presented as the winner of a competition is automatically viewed as a loser. So, when you have a group of children all competing with one another for one top prize, which includes the winner being presented to a cheering audience, and being showered with gifts and attention; feelings, self-esteem, and egos among other things, are bound to be bruised at the very least.

Do not get me wrong. I also understand that non-malicious competition is a part of life that is mostly enjoyable. And it is the responsibility of us as parents and adults to teach and prepare children to handle themselves graciously and respectfully, regardless of the outcome.

But we also have a responsibility as members of the body of Christ to use wisdom when it comes to presenting events within the church that can inadvertently do more harm than good.

The church is a spiritual hospital, and the youth ministry is the Pediatric Wing. There are many children (whether their parents are born-again believers or not) who come in wounded, broken, battered, and bruised with their heart-attacked, and suffering with emotional and spiritual fractures. These kids are in desperate need of (spiritual) treatment. We should follow Dr. Jesus' orders and render each patient's treatment in a form that is best fitting for him or her – to divert further endangerment away from the patient. When it comes to (spiritual) patients with compromised immune systems (a small amount or total lack of exposure to the word of God), we should also be careful not to further expose them to additional pathogens such as: rejection, insecurity, demeaning reprimands, embarrassment and alienation which could open the door to (spiritual) suicide.

Although I did not grow up in the church, my wife did. As a child, she suffered with many of the symptoms I previously mentioned. She was spiritually fragile and in search of acceptance and validation. But thank God for Dr. Jesus and those in the church that followed the personalized treatment plan He prepared just for her. She has been set free and is now a minister and a nurse, serving in the spirit and physical realms of healing and rehabilitation. It is always great when adults encourage and mentor children, but even greater when those same children go on to replicate our actions toward others.

I often prayed for God to reveal His purpose for my life, and order my steps so that I may do his will. It was at that time that God gave me the vision to start Guiding God's Children Sponsorship Program. This ministry would allow children of all ages to freely worship the Lord and honor Him with their God-given gifts and talents, while blessing others and glorifying the Kingdom of God – all at the same time! I was charged to host a youth talent showcase titled, *A Tribute to the King.* The talent showcase would be presented as an anointed, creative, encouraging, powerful, fun, and talent-packed environment that breaks the strongholds of alienation, low self-esteem, discouragement, insecurity, defeat, rejection, and fear.

Romans 16:20 says, *"The God of Peace will soon crush satan under your feet. May the grace of our Lord Jesus be with you"* (NLT). It is for this reason God has given me authority to bind the enemy and crush his plans to destroy God's family of tomorrow, by dismantling the children of today. However, the bible says that when we trust and obey God's word, no weapon turned against us will be successful, and every voice lifted to accuse us will be silenced. This scripture goes on to state that these benefits belong to, and are to be enjoyed by the servants of the Lord (Isaiah 54:17 NLT). So I'll make a long story short – we win!

Today, I am so grateful to God for helping me to recognize, unlock, and ignite the passion, purpose, and power that He placed inside of me. I thank God for everything He has brought me through, and brought me to. I now understand that I was being processed and prepared for my purpose – to help children and families to connect their passion and purpose with God's power to produce. To God be all the glory!

NOTES

_____

_____

_____

_____

_____

_____

_____

_____

_____

_____

_____

_____

_____

_____

CHAPTER 7

EMBRACE YOUR PURPOSE

One of the main characteristics of a trailblazer is one's passion to embrace his or her purpose. Many of you may be saying, "*I would have embraced my purpose by now, if only I knew what it was!*" A few of you may say, "*I know that I am gifted to do this and that, but I still don't know what my purpose is.*" And others may say, "*I know what my purpose is, but I'm having trouble walking it out.*" Well let's start from the beginning. Your passion ignites your purpose, your purpose is supported by your power (the Word of God), your power builds your faith, your faith strengthens your confidence, your confidence fuels your influence, and your influence catapults your prestige; which enlarges the Kingdom of God in the earth!

Put it this way, imagine your name is "**Purpose**" and you own a company called **Passion**. You, **Purpose**, are a reflection of your company, and never fail to go over and above what is expected of you to guarantee its success. You desire for everyone to be afforded the opportunity to access your life-changing *Multi-Purpose Problem Solving Solution,* and work hard to accomplish that goal. In the process, you learn that in order to expand and take your business global, you have to travel to a place called *Destiny*. You began your journey by purchasing a ticket with your company's credit card "*Word* Express." Its world-renowned status and borderless credit limit continues to boost your *faith* in its *power*. At each stop during your journey, you present *your **Multi-Purpose Problem Solving Solution** to everyone from CEOs, blue collar workers, Politian, the employed, the unemployed, rich, poor, men, women, all races, the churched, and the unchurched; to people of all ages and walks of life. You don't view anyone as unapproachable.

There are quite a few times during which you deal with unforeseen delays such as weather cancellations, missing a connection, last minute layovers, or mechanical problems that would have caused the average person to be content with how far they had come thus far, and simply return home. But not you! You may be delayed but refuse to be denied, because you are the epitome of the word relentless. It is your continuous enthusiasm and display of great *confidence* in your product and its validity that is undeniable, and fortifies your ability to **influence** anyone and everyone within earshot of your amazing presentation. And make no mistake, it is your God-given gift of **influence** that paved the way for your **prestigious** reputation to precede you, and brand your **Multi-Purpose Problem Solving Solution**, your company, as well as yourself – as unforgettable!

CONNECT YOUR PASSION AND PURPOSE WITH GOD'S POWER TO PRODUCE

One of the greatest gifts God afforded man was the gift of His Influential Anointing. The word *influential* means *"having the power (or authority) to cause changes."* One meaning for the word *anointing* is *"to officially or formally choose (someone) to do or be something."* Therefore, God officially chose man to reflect the Lord in the earth, and gave him the power (or authority) to cause changes (Genesis 1:26-28). As a result, man ruled the world – literally. On the other hand, man's authority was created and supervised by God. Nothing or no one else had the authority to steal, kill, or destroy it – not even man himself. The reason being, God is the creator and central source of all authority. And no one can create or destroy what God has already created and does not want destroyed.

The influential anointing that God transferred to man during creation was not destroyed during or after the fall of man. Although man disobeyed God and transferred the authority over to satan, God had a back-up plan and His name is Jesus! He is the *Anointed One*. Therefore, He was officially chosen by the Lord to remove burdens and destroy bondage from man as stated in the following, "*The Spirit of the Lord is upon me, because he hath anointed me to preach the gospel to the poor; he hath sent me to heal the brokenhearted, to preach deliverance to the captives, and recovering of sight to the blind, to set at liberty them that are bruised, 19) To preach the acceptable year of the Lord*" (Luke 4:18-19). Through His death, burial, and resurrection all power (authority) in heaven and earth was given to Him. He not only recovered God's delegated authority from satan; He also reinstated it back to man.

The influential anointing is just as present today as it was in the beginning. In this present day, the problem is not a lack of authority, but an ignorance of to whom that authority belongs. It belongs to God's righteous. Therefore, the present condition of the world and everything taking place in it is the fault and responsibility of man – not God. We all were created by God with His power to influence anything and everything at any given time. However, it is everyone's individual choice to do so in representation of God or the enemy. Think about it, man influences everything from animals, to machines, as well as one another.

Whether it be for good or bad, positive or negative, deliberate or subconscious, our lives are geared toward giving and receiving influence in some form or another. Regardless of who you are, where you come from, how much money you make, or what you have done in your past or present; your actions have exerted your ability to influence. Therefore, if ever there were a time for born-again believers in Christ to execute our influential authority for the glory of God, it would most certainly be now.

In other words, it is time to allow God to help you connect your passion and purpose with His power to produce – at any age or stage in your life! King Josiah, one of the greatest kings of Jerusalem, was only eight years old when he embraced God's purpose for his life and cleansed the nation of its idols and false Gods (2nd Chronicles 34:1). Abraham was seventy-five years old when he began to follow God and embrace his purpose as the "father of faith" (Genesis 12:4). Even in his old age, passed normal child bearing years, he was destined to become the "father of many nations" because of God's "super" joining with Abraham's "natural". He became the father of Ishmael, and was one hundred years old when his ninety-year-old wife Sarah gave birth to their promised son Isaac. As a result, the nation of Israel and many others were established. So, whether you are five or eighty-five, now is a great time to start walking in your purpose. If you are alive it is not too late.

Others may think, believe, or see your hopes and dreams as doubtful at best. But you need not concern yourself with the opinions of others, because they are completely irrelevant. Do not allow man's voice in your head to quiet the word of God in your heart. You were created a trailblazer, and trailblazers are innovative, secure, disciplined, and faith-filled individuals who boldly trust God and take refuge in the fact that whatever He has promised will come to past.

It is vital that you not only learn God's word, but believe it and allow it to guide you in every decision. Doing so will position you to be blessed beyond your wildest dreams, while blessing others in the process. As expressed through John 3:16, God really loves you more than you could ever imagine. He wants you to live and enjoy your purposeful life, and pursue your destiny with passion and precision despite critics, setbacks, or rocky-roads that may lie in your path. As my wife Renda always says, "R*ecognize your setbacks as set-ups for your comeback!*" Trust God and stay on course.

While trusting God and waiting on the manifestation of your dreams, visions, and desires to come to fruition, you have a Teacher, Guide, and Comforter – the Holy Spirit who will lead you. He is present with you always (John 14:16). He is to be your focal point as he reveals your purpose and leads you to your destiny. Keep in mind that you are more than qualified to successfully achieve what you are purposed to do. No person on earth or demon from hell should be able to discourage and convince you otherwise.

A great example of this is when satan tried to influence Jesus to completely change his course, by following His flesh instead of leading it as He always had, as stated in Matthew 4:3-4, "*And the tempter came to him, he said, If thou be the Son of God, command that these stones be made bread. 4) But he answered and said, It is written, Man shall not live by bread alone, but by every word that proceedeth out of the mouth of God.*" Jesus understood that not only was it important for Him to stay on His course, but the direction in which He traveled as well. The correct order was **God the father leading Jesus, and Jesus leading the flesh** as follows:

> ➢ flesh-> Jesus-> God the Father

Anything contrary would have been wrong. The enemy went on to try and further tempt Jesus, but of course he was unsuccessful. That was because Jesus knew that obeying God the Father by keeping the correct order in which to travel would be pivotal for man's survival. It would set the precedence for man to be victorious over sin and satan simultaneously. He knew the possibility of man spending eternity in Heaven or hell rested upon Him either relying on God's strength or surrendering to the weakness of His flesh. Unfortunately, satan often uses the same recycled tactics today with some success. It is because many people do not know or understand his strategy. The enemy's unsuccessful strategy toward Jesus was to:

1. Attack Jesus' identity and cause Him to doubt Who He was and to Whom He belonged.
2. Attack Jesus during a time in which He appeared to be isolated.
3. Attack Jesus during a time of physical weakness
4. Attack Jesus during a time in which the enemy expected Him to be physically, emotionally, and mentally vulnerable.
5. Attack Jesus by manipulating the word of God.

I can attest to this. Regrettably, there were times in which I was subjected to all of the above, and satan not only knew it, but also took full advantage of it. However, Jesus stayed on course. He did not allow the enemy to provoke Him to quickly make a hasty, permanent decision for a temporary problem. Jesus provided man's only chance of receiving God's complete redemption, salvation, and righteousness, which was His purpose for coming to earth. We must make it a habit to do as Jesus did and not allow any moment of solitude or weakness to cause us to abort God's purpose and destiny for our life. We must see it all the way through to its completion to be blessed, and more so to bless others.

When it comes to being a trailblazer, satan will always try to get you to veer off the course God predestined and placed you on. It is vital for you to not go to the left or right, but stay on your course! It is on your course that you are led by faith; not sight. No matter how foggy, awful, grim, bleak, discouraging and unpromising the atmosphere around you may appear, you must continue to be led by faith; not fear. We can take solace in the fact that God is incapable of misleading us. And if we stay on course and follow the Holy Spirit, we cannot be led by our flesh as stated in Galatians 5:16, *"So I say, let the Holy Spirit guide your lives. Then you won't be doing what your sinful nature craves"* (NLT).

The greatest and most relatable example of a trailblazer is Christ – hands down! He did not allow anyone or anything to distract, discourage, or deplete Him. He knew who He was, as well as to Whom He belonged. He was a total God pleaser! Ironically, he faced more resistance from His "peers" in the church than those outside of the church. But He never let it concern or persuade Him to follow or please them. He understood and embraced God's will for His life. And being the trailblazer that He is, Jesus dared to "swim-against-the-current" and embrace His individuality. This often resulted in rejection and alienation from his own kinsmen more so than strangers, but He was never surprised or intimidated by it. Jesus revealed this in the following scripture, *"A prophet has little honor in his hometown, among his relatives, on the streets where he played in as a child"* (Mark 4:6, MSG). However, Jesus did not allow their lack of honor to disrupt His honor for God. He did not stop going into the synagogues or respecting scripture because of the ungodly, religious behavior of some of its leaders and attendees. Neither did he complain about wrong doings that took place and cut himself off from everyone there. He understood that to do so would be counterproductive.

Instead, Jesus expressed to them the importance and great need for the word, love, and correction of God. And He did so with wisdom, compassion, patience, and forgiveness in a way in which no man before Him had done. Christ's method of operation was unorthodox yet credible; and appreciated by most. On the other hand, there were others, some of which were considered notable rabbis and scholars who openly and completely rejected Him. But even as Jesus rejected their pride, hypocrisy, narcissism, and vindictive ways, He did not allow His flesh to take control. He spoke the truth and encouraged change by will; not by force. He continuously did so without defecting from the word. Even when those closest to Him denied and deserted Him. He held steadfast to the word and the faith. He always walked with God, and God always walked with Him; even when it appeared He walked alone.

And so, being the trailblazer that you are, there will be times when you are following God and it appears that you are all alone. But nothing could be further from the truth! This would be the time in which you must doubt your doubt, and take refuge in the fact that God is always with you, as noted in Deuteronomy 31:8, "*Do not be afraid or discouraged, for the Lord will personally go ahead of you. He will be with you; he will neither fail you nor abandon you*" (NLT).

KNOW GOD'S VOICE

The following story is a very good example of why it is vital to know God's voice, regardless of whose voice He uses to speak through. Learning and obeying His voice is vitally necessary to successfully embrace and walk out your purpose. Failure to learn and obey God's voice can result in missed opportunities and blessing as stated in the following:

"I stood in my kitchen with my hands clenching my face. My hair was in golf with pain! I'll try to avoid taking medicine, so I decided to take a nap in hopes of sleeping my headache away. "Mom, let me tell you what happened to my friend Brittany today," my eleven-year-old daughter see it with excitement. I replied, "Not now baby I have a terrible headache. You can tell me about it later." Although disappointed, she obliged. She followed close behind me as I enter my bedroom. My headache escalated, so I decided to take some pain medication before lying down. To my disappointment, we were out of pain medicine. My daughter then said, "Mom, God wants..." I stopped her in mid-sentence, "Baby, please go play or watch TV. I feel terrible! I don't have time to listen to you right now."

Obviously, she looked at me and said, "I was only trying to help you." She then turned and left the room. After exhausting my natural ability, I prayed, "Lord, can you please heal my headache?" The Lord replied, "Sure, later" I cannot believe what I had heard. I asked, "Why later?" He replied, "Because you are too busy right now and you do not want to hear what I have to say." I said, "Oh no Lord, I'm never too busy for You." He said, "I tried to talk to you twice in the last 45 seconds but you would not listen." I could not remember hearing anything to me. I pondered over what had taken place 45 seconds prior. Finally, it came to me. I hurried out of my room, back into the hallway. I said to my 11-year-old, "I'm sorry for not listening to you. What did you want to tell me honey?" She said, "Brittany and I were playing in her guard, building seriously hurt her arm. She needed to see a doctor. I went along with Britney and her mom to the hospital. X-rays were taken, which confirmed a broken arm. As we all sat waiting for the doctor to put a cast on her arm, I put my hand on Britney's arm, I began to pray for her healing. As I ended the prayer, Brittney said the pain was gone and she could move her arm again! The doctor returned and said there have been a mistake. After looking at the x-rays a second and third time, her arm was not broken; only

bruised." I was speechless! My daughter went on to say,

"Mom, God says he's ready to heal you too, right now. He

wanted to do so earlier, but you didn't have time" (©2003

Renda Horne).

Just as the Mom in the previous story, many fail to receive what they desire from God. It is not always because they are not ready to receive, or because God is ignoring them; but can be quite the opposite. When it comes to communicating with God, many are often more focused on leading instead of interacting. As a result, they become seasoned "askers" but amateur "receivers" because they fail to actively listen when God gives them instructions that will lead to their blessings. And there are also those who want His blessings, but refuse to be inconvenienced by whatever process, participation, or sacrifice that may be required of them. They choose to forfeit their opportunity to receive from God; and therefore, remain unchanged.

In 2nd Kings 5:9-14, Naaman, a high-ranking official for the King, had leprosy. And although God was ready to heal him, Naaman's healing from Leprosy was delayed due to his pride and rejection of God's instruction. He went to see the prophet Elisha with expectations of speaking directly with him, and Elisha operating in a way Naaman felt would bring forth his healing. But instead, Elisha sent word by way of his servant to instruct Naaman to go and wash seven times in the Jordan River to receive his immediate and complete healing.

For Naaman, God's method of operation concerning his healing was a problem for three reasons: the first being that Elisha did not deliver the instructions to Naaman personally, and instead sent his servant. The second reason being that Naaman himself was required to activate his faith and participate actively participate in the process. And thirdly, the Jordan was dirty and unpleasant, and Naaman preferred an alternate, cleaner river in which to wash himself. And so, he stormed away angry with a bruised ego and still sick.

There are times like this in which people tend to blame God and others for their grim, and unchanged situation instead of the real culprit – themselves. James 2:26 states that faith without the proper corresponding actions; is dead. In this situation, it was Naaman's decision to refute God's instructions, and not proceed with the proper corresponding actions that would bring about what he was believing God for. Naaman's own pride, arrogance, inactivity, and disobedience blocked his healing; not God or Elisha. He did not receive his healing until he obeyed God and activated the proper corresponding actions. He received his blessing by listening, humbling himself, and obeying God's voice; regardless of who God spoke through, who He sent to instruct him, and what action he had to take for it to come forth. Naaman was not waiting on God, it was God who had been waiting on Naaman to humble himself and follow Him; instead of trying to lead.

Trailblazers walk in humility. They make themselves available to receive God's instruction and comply. They are never too busy for God. The fulfillment of His purpose for their life is top priority, instead of the other way around. The word of God is not only in their head, but also in their heart. They do not only talk faith; but live faith. No matter how out-of-the-box God's instructions may appear, they do not hesitate to comply because they know His voice.

KNOW YOUR ENEMY

The number one enemy of God, man, and all mankind is satan. Although I scratched the surface of the subject in a previous chapter, it is important that I go a little more in depth with his characteristics. This understanding would enhance the spiritual intelligence of a trailblazer (Proverbs 4:7), by unveiling why and how he continues to use the same recycled tactics and lies to wreak havoc in the earth.

The enemy already knows that he was defeated by Christ Jesus on our behalf. But if he can discourage people from hearing, believing, and capitalizing on this truth, he can possibly prevent man from maximizing the authority inherited from Christ's victory. Therefore, he continues to put up smoke screens to appear as though he is more powerful than God's anointed. 1st Peter 5:7 advises us to, *"Stay alert! Watch out for your great enemy, the devil. He prowls around **like** a roaring lion, looking for someone to devour"* (NLT, emphasis added). Take note that in the preceding scripture he is not stated as a lion, only his trying to **imitate** a lion. Not only is his power limited, but so is his time in the earth. The reason why he continues to fight a losing battle is because he is a loser who has nothing else to lose besides time.

It all began in Heaven. He was an angel named Lucifer who held the position of angelic worship leader. His position afforded him authority and great influence. He also had beauty, strength, and wisdom. At that time, he was sinless and his radiance prevalent (Ezekiel 28:13); and he was referred to as "lucifer, son of the morning" (Isaiah 14:12). He was responsible for leading all of God's angels in worship, as well as covering God (Ezekiel 28:14). However, all his beauty, splendor, wisdom, strength, and authority would be nullified when he decided to lift himself up with pride.

It was not satan's possession of beauty, splendor, wisdom, strength, and authority that led to him sinning, being stripped of it all, and expulsion from Heaven. It was when he executed his free will to allow those things to ultimately possess him instead. In other words, the enemy's demise was due to satan's acceptance and indulgence of sin by way of his own free will. God never intended to create *"robots,"* who He would mistreat and force them to worship Him. He created man with a "free will" that was meant to be a blessing; not a curse.

149

The Lord wanted and created angels and humans whom He would love and bless, and who would execute their individual free will to worship Him out of their love for Him as well. However, satan chose to use his free will to lift himself up with pride, and betray the Lord. One third of Heaven's angels chose to join with him to war against God. Needless to say, satan and his defecting angels were defeated. So, God stripped the devil of his position, authority, and beauty. He and his angels were then kicked out of Heaven for their sins of pride, jealousy, and treason against God (Luke 10:18). It was then that the enemy chose to escalate his madness. Being the fake he is, he decided to mimic God in any and everything he could. In a weak attempt to "appear" like the Most High God, he erected his kingdom of darkness above the stars, and has been trying to reroute the praises, honor, and glory due to the Most High God; toward his direction ever since (Isaiah 14:12-14).

It was God's creation of man in His own image, transfer of authority to man for a specific time frame, and unfailing love and redemption for man; was the spark that lit the fuse for satan's jealousy and hatred for man. That same contempt remains so to this day. As the Lord transferred His influential anointing to man in the Garden of Eden, satan looked on with anger, jealousy, and hatred for God, but even more so for man. This was because he understood that man now held the second most powerful and influential position under God Himself. And so, not only would satan be subject to God, but he would also be subject to man as well (Genesis 1:26-28).

KNOW YOUR "TRIGGERS"

Have you ever noticed how quickly your irritation level can spike in certain situations? Do you or someone you know find yourself getting irritated when the usher at church directs you to sit in an area that is completely opposite of where you would normally sit? Do you feel yourself getting irritated whenever your spouse is driving you to work, and feels the need to drive under the speed limit in the fast lane? Do you get irritated with others when they don't seem to be as passionate about a specific matter as you are? Do you get easily irritated when someone goes on and on about something you could really care less about? If so, it appears you have a "trigger" problem.

Triggers are things that provoke you to react in a manner that is mentally, physically, or emotionally hurtful, discouraging, and potentially deadly. They are often considered small barriers, but barriers none the less. A small "barrier" is like a small, sharp nail in the road. It may not stop you all at once, but it will certainly slow you down! I cannot stress enough the importance of identifying and taking authority over the deterrents, because denial can be deadly. A lack of control over triggers will cause you to become vulnerable to temptations of sin, and detour from the path God placed you on as stated here, *"When you follow the desires of your sinful nature, the results are very clear; sexual immorality, impurity, lustful pleasures, 22) envy, drunkenness, wild parties, and other sins like these. Let me tell you again, as I have before, that anyone living that sort of life will not inherit the Kingdom of God"* (Galatians 5:19-21 NLT). Triggers are to trailblazers, what kryptonite was to Superman – a thief! It robbed him of his ability to execute his purpose to its maximum level, put him in imminent danger.

Whenever there is an opportunity for you to apprehend peace during an episode of anger – take it

(Psalms 34:14). Just as important as it is for trailblazers to identify their triggers, it is equally critical for them to respond appropriately. The way in which you respond to your triggers can make all the difference between you being the blazing, blessed trailblazer that God desires; or a lukewarm, self-destructive blessing blocker. You should begin by repenting to God, and ask for His help. You should also examine and re-examine your thoughts consistently and adhere to the following scripture, *"And be not conformed to this world: but be ye transformed by the renewing of your mind, that ye may prove what is that good, and acceptable, and perfect, will of God."*

Furthermore, the following scripture gives us clear and precise instructions on how to handle our triggers. We are instructed, *"Therefore, since we are surrounded by such a huge crowd of witnesses to the life of faith, let us strip off every weight that slows us down, especially the sin that so easily trips us up. And let us run with endurance the race God has set before us"* (Hebrews 12:1 NLT).

The key to doing so is keeping your eyes focused on Jesus by engulfing yourself in the word of God, and being led by the Holy Spirit as stated in Galatians 5:16, *"So I say, let the Holy Spirit guide your lives. Then you won't be doing what your sinful nature craves"* and verse 5:25, *"Since we are living by the Spirit, let us follow the Spirit's leading in every part of our lives"* (NLT). Just as there are consequences for following the desires of your sinful nature, there are blessings that blossom in our lives as a result of following the Holy Spirit, *"But the Holy Spirit produces this kind of fruit in our lives: love, joy, peace, patience, kindness, goodness, faithfulness, 23) gentleness, and self-control. There is no law against these"* (Galatians 5: 22-23 NLT).

KNOW YOUR POWER

The enemy witnessed God frame the universe and much more by way of speaking His influence into the atmosphere. And as a result, it was so. The enemy also stood by and witnessed first-hand as God enjoyed the fruit of His labor, with man alongside Him duplicating God's power and success, *"And out of the ground the Lord God formed every beast of the field, and every fowl of the air; and brought them unto Adam to see what he would call them: and whatsoever Adam called every living creature, that was the name thereof"* (Genesis 2:19).

God had created some truly extraordinary things, but never anything like man before. Man was a spirit that was housed in flesh, and possessed authority in both the spiritual and physical worlds. The enemy realized that heaven and earth is literally influenced by every word man speaks. There are examples throughout the bible. Take for instance when Joshua spoke the word of God, and influenced the heavens (above the sky). The sun and the moon both submitted to his authority as stated here, *"On the day the Lord gave the Israelites victory over the Amorites, Joshua prayed to the Lord in front of all the people of Israel. He said, Let the sun stand still over Gibeon, and the Moon over the valley of Aijalon. 13) So the sun stood still and the moon stayed in place until the nation of Israel had defeated its enemies"* (Joshua 10:12-13 NLT). That scripture went on to say that on that day, the sun remained abnormally fixed in the middle of the sky as Joshua had spoken.

God is no respecter of person. No different from Joshua, Moses, or anyone else written of in the bible or elsewhere, the Lord desires for every person to accept and execute his or her God-given authority that Jesus spoke of in Luke 10:18-19 and Matthew 16:19. In spite of knowing what He would have to endure, Jesus had long anticipated coming to earth to fulfill the prophecy of Genesis 3:15. In fact, it was the very reason for His coming. He looked forward to destroying the works of enemy, and ensuring that man could live and enjoy life as God intended (John 10:10). Regardless of the chaos that may have erupted in your life today, victory is yours right now – through Jesus Christ. God can prepare you for triumph during tragedy, and prepare you for your purpose right in the middle of your pain. Know and believe that despite your rocky start, God can give you a smooth finish.

The following scripture was the fulfillment of the Genesis 3:15 prophecy God had spoken to the serpent in the Garden of Eden, *"Look, I have given you authority over all the power of the enemy, and you can walk among snakes and scorpions and crush them. Nothing will injure you"* (Luke 10:19 NLT). Through the bloodshed, death, burial, and resurrection of Jesus, satan was stripped of man's God-given authority. Man is again given the opportunity to reign on earth as a reflection of God in Heaven, and to live a "happy" (blessed, anointed to prosper) purpose-filled life here on earth, as it is in Heaven. As a result, I no longer face battles expecting victory; because I have been given the authority to possess victory at all times – and so can you.

GO, SOW, AND GROW!

In the beginning, God instructed man to be fruitful and multiply. Jesus fulfilled that scripture when he went into the world, sowed Himself, and the Kingdom of God increased in the earth. He then instructed the disciples to do the same, *"And he said unto them, Go ye into all the world, and preach the gospel to every creature"* (Mark 16:15). So, when you read the gospels, you witness "the making of a trailblazer" through the life of Jesus. You also see the training and duplication of that process through the lives of His disciples. Jesus instructs them to **Go** (into all the world), **Sow** (the word of God), and **Grow** (the Kingdom of God in the earth). The disciples completed their course and fulfilled their God-given purpose in the earth, just as Jesus, the King of all trailblazers had done. Now is your time to do as Jesus and **Go**, **Sow**, and **Grow**…Happy trails!

THE MAKING OF A TRAILBLAZER

BOOKING INFORMATION

If you are searching for a relevant and exciting speaker for your next life-changing youth conference, assembly, seminar, workshop, or event – search no more! Richard Horne Jr. will provide insightful life transitioning strategies, and tools, that can greatly impact, and inspire your attendees to turn their tragedies into triumph. Book Richard Horne Jr. today!

www.richardhornejr.com

Made in the USA
Columbia, SC
19 October 2024

44718716R00089